Handbook of Personal Evangelism

by

Dr. A. Ray Stanford
Founder of Florida Bible College

Pharr, Texas:
Wally Morillo
1991

Revised Edition 1975
Current Edition 1991
All material in this book can be quoted in part or in whole.
Reproduction is encouraged as there is no copyright.

Hope. Inspiration. Trust.

We're Social! Follow Us for New Titles and Deals:
FaceBook.com/CrossReachPublications
@CrossReachPub

Available In Paperback And eBook Editions
Please go online For More Great Titles
Available Through CrossReach Publications.
And If You Enjoyed This Book Please Consider Leaving A
Review On Amazon. That Helps Us Out A Lot. Thanks.

© 2016 CrossReach Publications
All Rights Reserved, Including The Right To Reproduce
This Book Or Portions Thereof In Any Form Whatever.

CONTENTS

FOREWORD 4

INTRODUCTION 4

CHAPTER I—The Message: God's Plan of Salvation 6

CHAPTER II – Eternal Security 13

CHAPTER III—Chastening and Rewards 15

CHAPTER IV—The Messenger 21

CHAPTER V—The Opening and the Close 28

CHAPTER VI—Repentance 36

CHAPTER VII—"Lordship Salvation" 39

CHAPTER VIII—Faith without Works 43

CHAPTER IX—Water Baptism 47

CHAPTER X – Evolution 51

CHAPTER XI—The Atheist and Agnostic 57

CHAPTER XII—The Jew 62

CHAPTER XIII—The Roman Catholic 71

CHAPTER XIV—20th Century Protestantism 77

CHAPTER XV—Jehovah's Witnesses 80

CHAPTER XVI—Seventh-Day Adventism 87

CHAPTER XVII—Christian Science and Unity 90

CHAPTER XVIII—Mormonism 94

CHAPTER XIX—Understanding the Two Natures 96

CHAPTER XX—Understanding Predestination 97

CHAPTER XXI—Helpful Hints 99

CHAPTER XXII—Literature: Recommended Reading List 102

CHAPTER XXIII—Illustration Illustrated 104

FOREWORD

This book places at your fingertips practical, clear, effective methods to reach people for Christ in a loving way. You will be provided the answers to difficult questions concerning cults, sects, religions, agnostics and atheists and how to recognize the truth from false doctrine.

You will have proof that creation is a scientific fact and that the theory of evolution is a farce. It will give you the know-how to give comfort and assurance to believers, that they can be saved for eternity and that God will never let them be lost. This book is dedicated to all who love people and don't want them to end up in hell.

Study to shew thyself approved unto God, a workman that needeth not to be ashamed, rightly dividing the word of truth. II Timothy 2:15

The Handbook of Personal Evangelism is the result of many years of study and active, effective soulwinning by Dr. A. Ray Stanford, Founder of Christian Youth Ranches; Grove Community Church; Florida Bible Church and Florida Bible College; Distinguished Flying Cross and Air Medal (twice) during World War II. This book was written with the assistance of Mrs. Carol Streib and Dr. Richard Seymour. The author expresses appreciation for proofreading the manuscripts to Mrs. Ann Patterson and Mrs. Connie Mitchell.

INTRODUCTION

THERE IS AN URGENT NEED FOR MEN AND WOMEN TO DEDICATE THEMSELVES TO THE IMPORTANT TASK OF BECOMING SPECIALISTS IN SOULWINNING!

SIMPLICITY

This book is written to guide a Christian in his personal witnessing so that he will present the plan of salvation in a clear and simple way that the lost can understand. To achieve simplicity in presenting the gospel takes much thought, much effort, and much practice. We must give the message in words the people can understand.

A doctor cannot communicate with most of his patients by using medical terminology. What the physician says may be true, but most patients will not be able to grasp the meaning. The Scriptures tell us in II Cor. 3:12, "Seeing then that we have such hope, we use great plainness of speech," and in I Cor. 14:8, 9, "For if the trumpet give an uncertain sound, who shall prepare himself to the battle? So like wise ye, except ye utter by the tongue words easy to be understood, how shall it be known what is spoken? For ye shall speak into the air."

Communication is with words, and they have to be on the level of the person's understanding. Christ said, "Feed My sheep." He did not say, "Feed My giraffes." As we prepare ourselves to reach a person for the Lord, we must constantly bear in mind how our words will come across to the lost. Remember, the average American cannot quote two Scriptures from memory. We do the lost a great injustice to speak in ecclesiastical terms which, though they may be precious to us, do not convey the proper meaning to the unsaved... and this defeats our whole purpose in witnessing.

Many people testify that before they were saved, although they went to church regularly and heard their minister use terms like "born again," "redemption," "justification," "propitiation," etc., they didn't understand that Christ had paid for all their sins on the cross. They didn't understand the gospel. It is a crime to keep people from coming to know the Lord as their Saviour because we felt like exhibiting our "30,000 word vocabulary."

Some may feel that a speaker is not "educated" unless he uses words the people cannot understand. They completely overlook the fact that to make something understandable takes much brilliance, thought, and work. As you strive to make the message plain, you will discover that "simplicity" is not simple... but it will greatly increase the fruit in your ministry.

WHY WE SHOULD WITNESS

1. THE NEED: God is real. Heaven is real. Hell is real. The Bible is the Word of God and tells us that all those who have not received Christ as their Saviour will spend eternity in hell... separated from God, in conscious torment (Luke 16:23-26; John

3:18). Knowing the terrible destiny of the unsaved should motivate anyone with any compassion at all to explain the plan of salvation to them. Paul said, "Knowing therefore the terror of the Lord, we persuade men..." (II Cor. 5:11).

I cannot understand how any person who really knows he will go to heaven when he dies could be so selfish as to keep the best news in the world from the lost who so desperately need Christ as their Saviour. It would be like not warning the sleeping occupants of a burning building of their great peril. To stand by and watch the building burn and let the people die in the flames would be a great and grievous sin. A woman once said to me, "I used to have a real burden for souls, but I have learned not to let it bother me, and now I just don't think about it any more." This person is a very busy church worker and is well thought of by her Christian friends. Do you think she is well thought of by God? I believe when we stand before the Lord Jesus Christ every Christian will wish he could call back the time and start witnessing as he should have while on earth, because then he will fully realize the need of souls for Christ as their Saviour. Now is the time to witness. Later will be too late.

2. GOD'S COMMAND: God has given every Christian a job, a responsibility, a command. "Go ye into all the world and preach the gospel to every creature" (Mark 16: 15). You can obey God's command, or you can disobey it. But your orders are still to WITNESS.

Remember, witnessing is a command of God, not a leading. God leads those who are already obeying His command to a particular field of service. Obey God's command of "GO" in the Scriptures! You don't stop your car when the signal light says, "GO!" "I charge thee therefore before God, and the Lord Jesus Christ... PREACH THE WORD; be instant in season, out of season..." (II Timothy 4:1,2). "For though I preach the gospel, I have nothing to glory of: for necessity is laid upon me; yea, woe is unto me, if I preach not the gospel!" (I Cor. 9:16).

If a father tells his son to mow the yard, and the son replies, "I don't feel led to... I'd rather watch television... but praise your name, Father, what is your will for me?" If my son said this to me, I would again tell him, "Go mow the yard!" If my son still didn't mow the yard, I assure you, it wouldn't be long until he would be in the "lawn-mowing business."

When you feel like it, and when you don't, you should consistently give out the gospel. We are in a battle for the souls of men. Soldiers cannot stop fighting on the battlefield just because they don't feel like fighting. God has chosen us to be soldiers for Him. There are enough "conscientious objectors." God is looking for loyal, front-line troops who will give themselves wholeheartedly to the task at hand... telling others the good news of salvation.

3. OUR PRIVILEGE: God could have chosen angels to carry the message of salvation-but He didn't. God gave every Christian the privilege and responsibility to be a carrier of the gospel. "But as we were allowed of God to be put in trust with the gospel, even so we speak; not as pleasing men, but God, which trieth our hearts" (I Thess. 2:4). "To wit, that God was in Christ, reconciling the world unto Himself, not imputing their trespasses unto them; and hath COMMITTED UNTO US the word of reconciliation" (II Cor. 5: 19).

Since God loved me enough to pay for my sins and give me eternal life, I certainly am not going to be ashamed of the gospel. Romans 10:17 says that "faith cometh by hearing and hearing by the Word of God." It is when people hear the gospel that they are saved. "For I am not ashamed of the gospel of Christ: for it is the power of God unto salvation to every one that believeth..." (Romans 1:16).

No Christian can claim inability to witness and blame God for it because the last words of Christ upon earth were, "But ye shall receive POWER, after that the Holy Ghost is come upon you: and ye shall be witnesses unto Me both in Jerusalem, and in all Judea, and in Samaria, and unto the Uttermost part of the earth" (Acts 1:8). As Christians, we already have the power, but sometimes we don't seem to want to use the power.

There is no greater joy than to lead a person to Christ. It is one of the many fruits God promises to those who obey Him. In addition to the peace of mind which comes from knowing we are doing as our Lord and Saviour has commanded us, God also promises rewards later on for the soul winner (Prov. 11:30; Dan. 12:3; I Thess. 2:19).

No book man could write could give you the desire to witness. Only the great love of God could constrain you to do so (II Cor. 5:14). Salvation is voluntary... you had to DECIDE to accept Christ as your Saviour. Service is also voluntary... you must DECIDE that the salvation of souls is worth disciplining your life.

It is our prayer that this book will give you concrete, practical suggestions on HOW to witness effectively.

"Herein is my Father glorified, that ye bear much fruit; so shall ye be My disciples" (John 15:8).

CHAPTER I—THE MESSAGE: GOD'S PLAN OF SALVATION

It would be wonderful if every person understood the entire Bible. There are many doctrines in the Bible that make extremely interesting topics of conversation. But in trying to lead a person to the Lord please remember that this person needs to understand the plan of salvation and nothing else until after he is saved.

God tells us that "...the natural man receiveth not the things of the Spirit of God; for they are foolishness unto him: neither can he know them, because they are spiritually discerned" (I Cor. 2:14). The unsaved cannot really grasp spiritual teachings because they are not born again and do not have the Holy Spirit within to teach them these things.

God wants the unsaved to trust Christ as their Saviour, and will deal with the unsaved and help them understand the verses on the plan of salvation (John 16:7-11). Wait until the person is saved before you start talking about service or any so-called "deeper" truths.

The following will help a person see his need of the Saviour and how he can be saved. Because of differences in religious upbringing, every person will not need the same degree of emphasis on each point. As you explain the plan of salvation to someone you will be sensitive to notice which areas he needs to have dealt with at some length.

First we will cover the doctrine, then we will discuss the presentation, throughout most of this book.

1. DOCTRINE—Everyone is a sinner, less perfect than God. "For all have sinned and come short of the glory of God" (Rom. 3:23). The Virgin Mary, the Pope, your minister, your mother, you and I...all are sinners. "For there is not a just man upon earth, that doeth good and sinneth not" (Ecc. 7:20).

"But we are all as an unclean thing, and all our righteousnesses are as filthy rags; and we all do fade as a leaf; and our iniquities, like the wind, have taken us away" (Isa. 64:6). If you compare your life with that of those around you, you might feel you are a good person; and, as man looks upon goodness, you may be. But when you compare even your best qualities with those of the Almighty God, you will immediately see that you are not as perfect as God. Nobody is. One word God uses when He says we "sin" is "hamartano" in the Greek, and means to "miss the mark" (James Strong's Concordance, page 10 of the Greek Dictionary of the New Testament, #264). We miss the mark of God's perfection.

PRESENTATION—Be careful how you point out the person is a sinner. Admit you are, and he will be much more willing to admit he is. An effective statement is, "God says everyone is a sinner...I am, you are, we all are." Some people associate the term "sinner" only with "vile criminals." Explain that when the Bible says we are sinners, it means even "good" people, because even they are not perfect. If you happen to know that the person is very moral, compliment him, but show that he still isn't perfect in God's sight (Isa. 64:6, James 2:10).

While we must never act like, or imply that, we are "holy" because of personal righteousness, neither is it wise to go to the other extreme. Don't tell him your past (or present) sins. Don't use phrases like, "I used to be a sinner, but now I am saved." A person will always be a sinner until he receives his glorified body. I have heard of a person who said he hadn't sinned in three years. I John 1:8 says, "If we say that we have no sin, we deceive ourselves, and the truth is not in us."

Sometimes a person will feel he is too great a sinner for Christ to save him. To such a person, an effective statement is, "God cannot save a good person!" (There are no good people...Rom 3:12.) When the person knows he is a sinner, don't badger him until he "loses face." Move on to the next thing you want him to see in the Bible.

ALWAYS keep the issue between the Bible and him and not between you and him. The issue isn't that you have the answers, but that God has the answers. Avoid referring to your opinion, that of his preacher, or of his denomination. Point out that "this is what the Bible says.")

2. DOCTRINE—The result and penalty of sin is death...separation from God. "For the wages of sin is death..." (Rom. 6:23). The payment for sin is death. Sin is not paid for by good works, penance, church membership, water baptism, etc. Sin is paid

for by death. God does not hate the sinner, but He hates the sin. He hates sin because it separates us from Him (Isa. 59:2), and He doesn't want us to be separated from Him. "In flaming fire taking vengeance on them that know not God and that obey not the gospel of our Lord Jesus Christ: Who shall be punished with everlasting destruction from the presence of the Lord and from the glory of His power" (II Thess. 1:8,9).

Except for those taken in the Rapture, everyone will die physically. The body goes back to dust, and the soul goes to heaven or hell. Everyone is born dead spiritually (Eph. 2:1). The soul is separated from God because we are sinners. This is why Christ said in John 3:7, "...Ye must be born again." Only through a new birth of the Spirit can man have eternal life. If a person dies without having trusted Christ as his Saviour, his soul will be separated from God and he will ultimately be cast into the lake of fire forever...the Bible calls this the "second death" (Rev. 20:14,15).

PRESENTATION—For most people, a simple statement on this point is sufficient, as: "God loves us but hates our sin, because the payment for sin is death and separation from Him." How to deal with specific "cult teachings" that differ from Scripture on this point will be covered in the chapters on Jehovah's Witnesses and Christian Science. When you do not sense resistance on this point (and you usually won't), move on to what you want to cover next.

3. DOCTRINE—The eternal heaven will be a perfect place. No sin could enter this heaven. Man must be perfectly righteous to go to heaven. "Nevertheless we, according to His promise, look for new heavens and a new earth, wherein dwelleth righteousness" (II Peter 3:13).

"And there shall in no wise enter into it anything that defileth, neither whatsoever worketh abomination, or maketh a lie: but they which are written in the Lamb's book of life" (Rev. 21:27). "For thou art not a God that hath pleasure in wickedness: neither shall evil dwell with thee" (Psalm 5:4).

It is God's heaven. He created it (Gen 1:1). He lives in it (Psalm 11:4; 115:3). He says there will be no tears, sorrow, pain or death in heaven (Rev. 21:4), and God has the right to say who will go there. If any sin were allowed into heaven, death would be there because, as we have seen, "The wages of sin is death.." (Rom. 6:23).

Not only are we sinners and need our sin paid for before we can enter heaven, but also this body we have now could never live forever anyway. It will get old, sickly, and die. This body was never created to live forever. In the commercial world they call this "planned depreciation." This is why your car, washing machine, lawn mower, etc., need repairs and finally just won't operate.

God not only offers a payment for your sin so your soul can go to heaven, but He also will give you a new, glorified body that will live forever, entirely free from sin, sickness, and death. It will be like the glorified body of our Lord Jesus Christ (Phil. 3:21; I John 3:2).

PRESENTATION—When a person sees that he is a sinner and that with his sin he cannot enter heaven, he will be ready for the next point. Usually a statement like "Heaven is a perfect place, and no sin can enter heaven because sin would bring death" will be sufficient.

4. DOCTRINE—Nothing man could do could help him obtain the absolute perfection God requires for eternal life. "For by grace are ye saved through faith; and that not of yourselves: It is the gift of God: Not of works, lest any man should boast" (Eph. 2:8,9).

"But to him that worketh not, but believeth on Him that justifieth the ungodly, his faith is counted for righteousness" (Rom. 4:5).

'Knowing that a man is not justified by the works of the law, but by the faith of Jesus Christ, even we have believed in Jesus Christ, that we might be justified by the faith of Christ, and not by the works of the law, for by the works of the law shall no flesh be justified." (Gal 2:16).

"Not by works of righteousness which we have done, but according to His mercy he saved us..." (Titus 3:5).

"Therefore we CONCLUDE that a man is JUSTIFIED BY FAITH, without the deeds of the law" (Rom. 3:28).

If anything is clear in Scripture, it is that man is saved by his faith in Christ's payment for all sin on the cross plus nothing. Man's efforts, no matter how good or well intended (before or after salvation), have nothing to do with it. Salvation is by the finished work of Christ and nothing can be added to it.

Religions are man made. Two Latin words make up our English word "religion;" "re" and "ligio." "Re" means to "go back," and "ligio" means "to bind." "Religion" then means "to bind back." Religions are man's efforts to bind himself back to God. They are Satan inspired. Satan delights to blind man into thinking he could somehow earn eternal life through his good works. "And no marvel; for Satan himself is transformed into an angel of light. Therefore it is no great thing if his ministers also be transformed as the ministers of righteousness..." (II Cor. 11:14,15). People have Satan pictured as having horns, tail, pitchfork, and wearing a red union suit. Satan doesn't want people to know what he is really like.

The plan of salvation is not a religion but is the message of what God has already done to bring us back to Him. Satan gives the lost a religion that, when he hears it, will blind him to salvation. When you witness, always point out that the GOSPEL is NOT a "religion." We are not discussing man's philosophy but God's Word.

It is often very valuable to point out that you do believe in freedom of worship without persecution. Nevertheless, all the religious leaders of the world are dead: Buddha, Confucius, Mohammed, Mary Baker Eddy, etc. But the Lord Jesus Christ is alive! He is not dead! It would behoove those who want to come back from the dead to listen to the Man who did.

That a person cannot save himself by his works...or help Christ to save him by his works...or help keep himself saved by his works, will be one of the most difficult things for a person to believe. It is also one of the most IMPORTANT things for a person to believe...because if a person does not believe this, he is not saved. God says you are not saved by your works but by grace through faith.'

"And if by grace, then is it no more of works: otherwise grace is no more grace. But if it be of works, then is it no more grace: otherwise work is no more work" (Rom. 11:6).

GOOD WORKS FOR SALVATION IS SATAN'S COUNTERFEIT OF GOD'S GRACE FOR SALVATION. THIS ISSUE OF "GRACE versus WORKS" WILL ALMOST ALWAYS BE THE MAIN THING YOU WILL NEED TO DEAL WITH. HOW TO OVERCOME THIS SATANIC BARRIER WILL BE DISCUSSED THROUGHOUT THIS BOOK.

Satan does not want the lost to sin. He wants them to be fine, well-educated, well-liked, moral, religious people. It is a better advertisement for him. He offers them a "heavenly" way to go to hell.

God says in Matt. 7:21-23, "Not every one that saith unto Me, Lord, Lord, shall enter into the kingdom of heaven; but he that doeth the will of My Father (I Tim. 2:3, 4) which is in heaven. Many will say to Me in that day, Lord, Lord, have we not prophesied in Thy Name? And in Thy Name have cast out devils? And in Thy Name done many WONDERFUL WORKS? And then I will profess unto them, I NEVER knew you; depart from Me, ye that work INIQUITY."

These people tried to work their way to heaven, and God called it SIN. When a person realizes that even the best he can possibly do is still filthy rags in God's sight (Isa. 64:6), he should see the utter folly of believing his good works could help save him.

PRESENTATION—The way to overcome this false teaching that man needs to do good works for salvation is to present the person with the clear statements in the Word of God on salvation by faith alone without works. Sometimes you will need to use only a few verses. Great! But often, because people have been so misled and actually blinded by a counterfeit "Christian-do-good-religion," you will have to go over and over salvation-by-faith verses.

AN IMPORTANT THING TO REMEMBER—Do not let the person get off onto side issues. Stay with the gospel. What is the power of God unto salvation? Yes, the gospel. Satan will constantly work to get you to leave the gospel.

If a person insists that he must work for salvation, show him verses like Eph. 2,8,9, and stay with them. Ask "How would you interpret 'NOT OF WORKS'—that it is of works? God says it is NOT of works." You will not have a problem so much with a person's interpretation of Scripture as with his belief of Scripture. Some people are just unwilling to accept what God says at face value. This is calling God a liar and is so serious that it will result in the person's going to hell.

5. DOCTRINE—Christ made a complete payment for all sin and offers His righteousness. "For He (God) hath made Him (Christ) to be sin for us, who knew no sin; that we might be made the righteousness of God in Him" (II Cor. 5:21). Christ never sinned. He lived a perfect life. Yet He took our sins upon Himself and paid for them. He did this so He could give us God's righteousness in place of our sin.

"All we like sheep have gone astray; we have turned every one to his own way; and the Lord hath laid on Him the iniquity of us all" (Isa. 53:6). We are all sinners. We do what we want to do. But God allowed Christ to take our sin upon Himself and pay for it ALL.

"For Christ also hath once suffered for sins, the Just for the unjust, that He might bring us to God, being put to death in the flesh, but quickened by the Spirit" (I Peter 3:18). Christ was the Just One, We are the sinners. But He came to earth, took on flesh, died on the cross, and rose from the dead, so that we could live forever in heaven with the Lord.

"Who His own self bare our sins in His own body on the tree, that we, being dead to sins, should live unto righteousness: by whose stripes ye were healed" (I Peter 2:24). Jesus paid for our sins by Himself. He needed no help. We were dead spiritually because of our sins; but He died so we could be alive spiritually, because He would give us His righteousness. We are made whole because He took our punishment.

"And you, being dead in your sins and the uncircumcision of your flesh, hath He quickened together with Him, having forgiven you all trespasses; blotting out the handwriting of ordinances that was against us...and took it out of the way, nailing it to His cross" (Col. 2:13, 14). You were spiritually dead; you became spiritually alive when you trusted His payment for your sin. He then forgave you all trespasses. He can forgive us because He took all our sins and paid for them.

"Who gave Himself for us, that He might redeem us from all iniquity..." (Titus 2:14).

"Be it known unto you therefore, men and brethren, that through this Man is preached unto you the forgiveness of sins: And by Him all that believe are justified from all things, from which ye could not be justified by the law of Moses" (Acts 13:38, 39). Keeping the law could not save you. But Christ paid for all sin; so, if you believe in Him, He will forgive you and justify you from all the wrong you have done.

"By the which will we are sanctified through the offering of the body of Jesus Christ, once for all. For by one offering He hath perfected forever them that are sanctified" (Heb 10:10,14). It is God's will that we are made pure and holy because Jesus offered Himself for our sins. His ONE payment was sufficient for all sins, of all time, for all people. By this ONE offering we who believe are made perfect forever. We are pure and holy through His death.

Had Christ not fully paid for all sin, we could not receive justification and He would not have come back from the dead (Rom. 4:25). Since the payment for sin is death, He would still be in that grave. But Christ is risen from the dead, proving God is satisfied with the payment for sin that Christ made.

The Jews...the Romans...Pilate...who killed Christ? Who is guilty of His death? Jesus Himself told us no man TOOK His life. Listen to His words, "...I lay down My life, that I might take it again. No man TAKETH it from Me, but I lay it down of Myself..." (John 10:17, 18). I am as guilty of His death as anyone else. He died for me. He died to pay the price of my sin.

Why did Christ come to earth? To live? Or to die? "For even the Son of man came not to be ministered unto, but...to give His life a ransom for many (Mark 10:45). A ransom is a price paid to free someone from captivity. Christ died to pay the full price of our sin to free us from our captivity to the satanic wages of our sin—spiritual death. Sin is completely paid for.

What do we lack? We lack righteousness. God is anxiously waiting to give us His righteousness. God gives His righteousness to whoever accepts Christ's payment for their sin...and He gives His righteousness the moment the person accepts Christ (II Cor. 5:21). The righteousness of God is given only by faith—never by works (Rom 4:5-8; 4:22-24; 9:30-32).

PRESENTATION- Since this is the heart of the gospel, you should carefully go over the verses teaching Christ paid for all sin. If the person does not accept the teaching of Scripture at first, reiterate trying to make the verses as clear to the person as you can. (A very effective gesture in making the plan of salvation clear, and especially on this point, is explained and illustrated in Chapter 23.) When the person sees that "Jesus Paid It All," go on to the next point.

6. DOCTRINE—All man must do to be saved is to BELIEVE Jesus was the Lord who paid for all his sin—RECEIVE Christ as his Saviour. God gives eternal life only to those who will accept it by faith alone.

John 33:16, "For God so loved the world, that He gave His only begotten Son, that whosoever believeth in Him should not perish, but have everlasting life." Notice it is not to those who try to work and earn their eternal life but to those who believe.

John 6:47, "Verily, verily, I say unto you, He that believeth on Me HATH everlasting life." Christ who never told one lie, emphasized by saying, Truthfully, truthfully, he that believes on Me possesses now everlasting life.

John 1:12, "But as many as received Him, to them gave He power to become the sons of God, even to them that believe on His Name." Salvation is always RECEIVING. We do nothing We accept what Christ has done for us. We RECEIVE Him as our Saviour.

John 6:28,29, "Then said they unto Him, What shall we do, that we might work the works of God? Jesus answered and said unto them, This is the work of God, that ye believe on Him whom He hath sent." GOD did the work. God only asks of us that we believe on Christ.

Philippians 3:9, "And be found in Him, not having mine own righteousness, which is of the law, but that which is through the faith of Christ, the righteousness which is of God by faith." Notice, found in Christ—not in the Pope, your church, your denomination, or your own philosophy. You are found "in Christ" not by trying to get to heaven by your own righteousness, but by receiving Christ's righteousness by faith. God counts you righteous because of your faith not because of your works (Rom. 4:5).

We quoted Ephesians 2:8,9 earlier in this chapter, and now we shall examine it phrase by phrase.

For by grace: By mercy from God that we do not deserve.

Are ye saved: Not helped, instructed but "saved."

Through faith: Not through your church, through yourself, or anything else. Just through your faith.

And that not of yourselves: Not by what you do- regardless.

It is the gift of God: It is a gift. It is not sold for any price. The price would be too high. God could never lower the wages of sin. You cannot buy your way (I Pet. 1:18, 19). You accept salvation as God's gift or you cannot have salvation.

Not of works: Doesn't mean Jesus did a lot and you will help Him some. "Not of works" means NOT of works!

Lest any man should boast: God doesn't want any braggarts in heaven, and there won't be any braggarts there (I Cor. 1:29). All praise will be to the Lord Jesus Christ.

Galatians 3:22-26, "But the Scripture hath concluded all under sin that the promise by faith of Jesus Christ might be given to them that believe." Everyone is a sinner, and God promises to save those who have faith and believe in Jesus.

v. 23, "But before faith came, we were kept under the law, shut up unto the faith which should afterwards be revealed." Before you trusted Christ, you thought salvation was through keeping the law.

v. 24, "Wherefore the law was our schoolmaster to bring us unto Christ, that we might be justified by faith." The law showed how short you came of perfection, so you saw your need of Christ as Saviour.

v. 25, "But after that faith is come, we are no longer under a schoolmaster." When you trusted Christ by faith, the law had served its purpose. It is done away with as far as you are now concerned (II Cor 3:6-11).

v. 26, "For ye are all the children of God by faith in Christ Jesus." You become a child of God through your faith in Christ, and He will take care of you.

Romans 5:1, "Therefore being justified by faith, we have peace with God through our Lord Jesus Christ." Since I trusted Christ, God sees me justified—"just as if I'd never sinned." God sees Christ's righteousness instead of my sin. Therefore I have peace with God. Jesus reconciled God and me (Romans 5:8-11).

Acts 13:38,39, "Be it known unto you therefore, men and brethren, that through this man is preached unto you the forgiveness of sins: And by Him all that believe are justified from all things, from which ye could not be justified by the law of Moses." Through Christ you are justified from all things—past, present, and future. This is very important. "Jesus paid it ALL!" You could not be justified through keeping the law. ("Therefore by the deeds of the law there shall no flesh be justified in His sight..." Romans 3:20) Do not despise God's grace. Do not reject God's grace. If you could have been saved through your own efforts, Christ's death would have been useless. Calvary would have been a mistake. "I do not frustrate the grace of God: for if righteousness come by the law, then Christ is dead in vain" (Gal. 2:21). Going back to Acts 13:39, notice that those who are justified from all things are those who BELIEVE.

PRESENTATION—Since the greatest majority of those you meet are trying to somehow "work their way" to heaven, it will follow that the are not trusting Christ alone for their salvation. It is important to remember as you deal with them that they probably have never REALLY understood the gospel. Most churches that are "Christian" in name do not make the plan of salvation clear; some do not even know what the plan of salvation is to begin with.

Praise God for the godly pastors who stand for the Word of God!

Millions of people are so fed up with this counterfeit type of Christianity they have heard all their life from Sunday School days on up, that they do not even want to discuss "religion." Sympathize with them. Explain that what you want to talk about is not a religion. Explain the gospel to them. But do not insinuate that they are "stupid," etc. Remember, they do not know the truth.

(Sometimes it will be easier to lead to the Lord those who have rejected "religion," because at least they have recognized something was not "right" about what they had been taught. Compliment them on their insight. Agree with people wherever you can.)

Again the issue is between "grace and works." Until they see that Christ's death completely paid for their sin, they will not be ready to rely on that payment alone naturally. Keep showing them the verses, and get them to see that this is what God has to say about the matter.

Sometimes a person will question your authority to speak on theological issues. Explain to him that it is not a question of his opinion versus yours. You are showing him what GOD has said. HE is the authority. At the same time, if you are dealing with a true intellectual, comment on his obvious intelligence, and use this as a means to his salvation: Mention that with such brains and reasoning power as he has, he ought to see right away that the only way sinners could be saved would be the way God has explained in the Bible.

When the person trusts Christ as his Saviour, it is always important to explain to him then that he can know he has eternal life from that moment on, which is the last point we will cover in this chapter.

7. DOCTRINE—Man can know he has eternal life now because eternal life IS eternal. "For the wages of sin is death; but the gift of God is ETERNAL LIFE through Jesus Christ our Lord" (Rom. 6:23). Notice, the gift of God is ETERNAL LIFE-not, "life until you sin again," nor "life until you backslide."

Notice what John 3:16 is saying, "For God so loved the world that He gave His only begotten Son, that whosoever believeth in Him should not perish but have EVERLASTING LIFE." How long is EVERLASTING? Is it six months? Ten years? Does it start and stop? No! Everlasting life is FOR EVER AND EVER!

God's gift is SALvation...not PRObation. God's gift is eternal life...not temporary life.

John 6:47 has been quoted before showing you only need to believe. But what does this believing do for you? "Verily, verily, I say unto you, he that believeth on Me hath EVERLASTING LIFE." "Hath everlasting life" is present tense. If you have EVERLASTING LIFE right now, you are safe forever. You do not wait until you die to receive everlasting life. You receive it the instant you trust Christ as your Saviour.

I John 5:13, "These things have I written unto you that believe on the Name of the Son of God; that ye may know that ye have ETERNAL LIFE, and that ye may believe on the Name of the Son of God."

This is written to a certain class of people-not to the rich or poor, American or African, Jew or Gentile, Buddhist or Baptist-but to those who believe on the Name of the Son of God. His name is Jesus. "Jesus" comes from he Greek translation of the Hebrew words "Jehovah Yasha" and means "the eternal, self-existent God who saves and keeps."

Those who believe Jesus is the Lord and trust Him to save them and keep them saved can KNOW they have ETERNAL LIFE. You do not need to hope, think, guess, or pray for it. You can KNOW you have it.

AND WHEN GOD PROMISES YOU CAN KNOW YOU HAVE ETERNAL LIFE, YOU CAN COUNT ON IT, BECAUSE GOD CANNOT LIE (Titus 1:2).

PRESENTATION-After you have gone over what the name "Jesus" means, ask the person, "Is this written to you? Do you believe on the Name of the Son of God?" Once the person actually receives Christ as his Saviour, there should be no difficulty for him to realize he now has eternal life. Heaven is the tremendous inheritance of the children of God, and for a Christian to lack the full assurance of knowing he will go to heaven when he dies would be a great tragedy.

Those who do not know they will be saved forever are usually not saved to start with. The first section of Chapter Two will go into how to deal with a person lacking assurance of salvation.

Chapter Five deals with how to give a person the "invitation" to trust Christ as his Saviour.

Below are listed salvation verses which would be of great benefit to you to have memorized. You should memorize most of them so well that you could quote them readily. Know the address of where they are in the Bible so that you can turn to them quickly. The reasons for memorizing these verses are many:

(1) You can have the person read the verse, and you will be free to watch his eyes and expressions as he reads. For you to know his reaction as he reads will help you witness to him further.

(2) You might not have your Bible with you when you have the opportunity to witness, so you will need to quote the verses.

(3) Knowing the Scriptures this well will give you confidence as you witness. It is the Word of God that the Holy Spirit blesses. When you know the Scriptures, you will be amazed at how the Lord will bring just the right ones to your mind that will fit the need of the person.

MEMORY VERSES FOR CHAPTER ONE

* Romans 3:23
Isaiah 64:6
* Romans 6:23
Ephesians 2:1
II Peter 3:13
Revelation 21:27
I John 3:2
* Ephesians 2:8,9
* Romans 4:5
* Galatians 2:16
* Romans 3:28
Romans 11:6
* II Corinthians 5:21
* Isaiah 53:6
I Peter 3:18

I Peter 2:24
Titus 2:14
Hebrews 10:10,14
Mark 10:45
* John 3:16
* John 6:47
* John 1:12
John 6:28,29
* Philippians 3:9
Galatians 3:22-26
Romans 5:8-11
* Acts 13:38,39
* I John 5:10-13
Titus 1:2

Note: If you are unaccustomed to memorizing Scripture, we recommend you start with the verses marked *.

CHAPTER II – ETERNAL SECURITY

Eternal security is not a separate doctrine from salvation.
If you are not saved forever, you are not saved.

Those who think they are saved now but could lose their salvation later, have one of two problems: (1) either they are trusting to some degree in their works to save them, or (2) they do not understand that by trusting Christ as their Saviour, their destiny is in God's hands. Perhaps they have had little or no Bible teaching and do not realize that God has determined that all who believe will go to heaven when they die.

The first group, those who think leading a poor Christian life will result in a loss of their salvation, actually need to have the plan of salvation made clear to them. Somewhere they have not fully understood that Christ's death paid for ALL their sin, that their works have NOTHING to do with their salvation, and that only their FAITH IN CHRIST will save them. You would answer their questions just as you would almost any lost person's; it is a clear-cut problem of "grace and works." You just stay with the gospel until they see the light.

An illustration that has clarified the issue for many with this problem deals with the definition of the word "Saviour." What is a Saviour? Suppose you are drowning. There you are out in the middle of the ocean. Suppose someone were to throw you a book, Three Easy Lessons on How to Swim. Would he be a Saviour? No! Perhaps he could be called an "educator."

Now suppose a man got out of his boat, jumped in along side you, and demonstrated various swimming strokes showing you just how you ought to do it. Would he be a Saviour? Of course not. He would merely be an "example."

All right, what if he took you into his boat, dried you off, fed you, took you ten miles from shore-and then threw you out again into the ocean? Would he be a Saviour? By all means, no! He would be as a "deceiver," a "probation officer," one who starts a heroic act and then quits right in the middle. He certainly would not be a Saviour!

A Saviour is one who takes you safely all the way to shore! When God says He gives you eternal life and that He will never cast you out or lose you, He means it because He is the true Saviour! If you do not trust Christ to take you all the way to heaven, then you have not trusted Him as your Saviour. Let's examine Christ's own promise in John 6:37, "All that the Father giveth Me shall come to Me; and him that cometh to Me I will in no wise cast out." He says those who come to Him will not be cast out for any reason.

To bring home this truth, use an illustration from family life. What kind of a parent would you be if, when your child was disobedient, you kicked him out and said, "Go to hell, I'm through with you!" Rather, the proper parent says, "Come on in!" and the parent has ways and means to deal with the disobedient child.

God never casts out His children! God has other ways and means to deal with them, which we will discuss in Chapter Three.

Some would say, "All right, God won't cast me out, but I could get out of my own will and choice." The Lord anticipated such doubts and answers them clearly in John 6:39, "And this is the Father's will which hath sent Me, that of all which he hath given Me I should lose nothing, but should raise it up again at the last day." It is God's will that no saved person would ever become lost. He says He will "lose nothing," and you are at least something! You could never be saved and lost again. God saves you forever. This is HIS will!

In witnessing you should use only as many verses as are necessary for the person to see the truth. (Too many verses will confuse the person.) On this point of not losing salvation, you will usually find that John 6:37 and 6:39 are sufficient. They are certainly clear. At times you might sense that certain cases require additional verses, and the Scriptures abound with clear teaching. Study the passages thoroughly so you will know which verses will best answer the need of the person. I Peter 1:4, 5, "To an inheritance incorruptible, and undefiled, and that fadeth not away, reserved in heaven for you, who are kept by the power of God through faith unto salvation ready to be revealed in the last time." Notice who is keeping our salvation... God Himself, by His own almighty power! And He is reserving place in heaven for us.

I Cor. 6:19, "What? Know ye not that your body is the temple of the Holy Ghost, which is in you, which ye have of God...?" The Holy Spirit lives inside of every believer. John 14:16, 17 says, "And I will pray the Father, and He shall give you another Comforter, that He may abide with you forever; even the Spirit of truth... for He dwelleth with you, and shall be in you." The Holy Spirit is in believers forever. If a saved person could go to hell, the Holy Spirit would have to go to hell, too.

Eph. 1:13, 14, "In whom ye also trusted, after that ye heard the Word of truth, the gospel of your salvation: in whom also after that ye believed, ye were sealed with that Holy Spirit of promise, which is the earnest of our inheritance until the redemption of the purchased possession, unto the praise of His glory." The Holy Spirit indwells every believer from the moment he trusts Christ as his Saviour for evermore. One important reason for this is to keep us saved and protected until we receive our glorified body. The term "earnest of our inheritance" is like when we make a "down payment on a house." It is a guarantee that the rest is coming later-now we have the new birth-later we will have our new body.

I Cor. 12:27, "Now ye are the body of Christ, and members in particular." The moment you are saved, you become a member of the body of Christ. If you could ever become unsaved, part of Christ's own body would go to hell.

John 10:28, "And I give unto them eternal life; and they shall never perish, neither shall any man pluck them out of My hand." Notice again that Christ gives eternal life, and they who receive this eternal life shall never perish! When you look up the word "never" which occurs in John 10:28 in Strong's Concordance, you find that it comes from five different Greek words which are spelled in English: OU, ME, EIS, HO, and AION. The words OU and ME form a double negative meaning "Not at all, by no means, in no case, never." This double negative was used to state denials or prohibitions emphatically (Dana and Mantey, A Manual Grammar of the Greek New Testament, p. 266). The remaining three words combine to form an idiomatic expression meaning "forever" (The Englishman's Greek New Testament, p. 276).

When you put all of these meanings together, you find that when Christ says "never" here in this verse it carries with it very powerful assurance-much more than one word "never" ordinarily carries with it in our minds. If we were to take this most emphatic way of saying "never" in the Greek and try to bring it across into the English, John 10:28 would read something like this: "And I give unto them eternal life and they shall not at all, by any means, male or female, in any case, forever perish."

Christians are sanctified through the death of Christ (Heb. 10:10), and Hebrews 10:14 tells us, "For by one offering He hath perfected forever them that are sanctified." Believers are sanctified, and Christ gives them the perfection they need to go to heaven. The word "sanctified" means to be made "holy, pure and blameless" (Strong's Concordance, Greek #37). God would never send a believer to hell... He has made the believer holy and blameless and has given him a perfection which will last FOREVER.

John 5:24, "Verily, verily, I say unto you, He that heareth My word, and believeth on Him that sent Me, hath everlasting life, and shall not come into condemnation; but is passed from death unto life." Christ says those who have everlasting life (they already have it) shall not be condemned (promise for the future). Since God promises believers will not be condemned, why not take Him at His Word and realize they will not be condemned? Believers cannot go to hell: They have already "PASSED from death unto life"!

Philippians 3:9, "And be found in Him, not having mine own righteousness which is of the law, but that which is through the faith of Christ, the righteousness which is of God by faith." Christ's own righteousness is given to believers. Who would dare say Christ's righteousness isn't good enough for heaven?!?

Colossians 2:13 and Acts 13:39 say the believer is already justified and forgiven of all sins. So what sin could send you to hell? In fact, when Christ died on the cross for our sins, ALL our sins were future. Romans 8:28-39 teaches nothing can separate believers from God. HE justified us; nobody could charge a single thing against us! What a Saviour we have!

I John 5:10-13 is as clear a passage as could be written. Christ's death on the cross does not do anything for you unless it gives you everlasting life. If you have Christ as your Saviour, you have this life. Anyone who doubts that God gives eternal life is calling God a liar. Don't you think it would be very unwise to call God a liar? Personally, I wouldn't want to be in that category.

There is an illustration which you might find will interest people along this subject. One evening a man was having trouble with doubts about his salvation. His wife came into the bedroom and found her husband running his Bible back and forth under the bed, and she asked him what in the world he was doing. He said he knew Satan was in the darkest places, so he was showing Satan I John 5:13! (And this is a good idea when you have a doubt. Just claim the promise from the Word of God, and Satan will have no ground to give you doubts any more. The Word of God silences Satan.)

Since God tells me I can know I have eternal life, I say, "Thank you!" and I know I have eternal life. I am taking God at His Word. God said it... I believe it... that settles it! I base my whole eternity on the fact that God cannot lie and His Word cannot fail.

"God is not a man, that He should lie... hath He said, and shall He not do it? Or hath He spoken, and shall He not make it good?" (Numbers 23:19)

You will discover that when a person really understands the plan of salvation, he rarely will have a problem with "eternal security." It has been our experience that the most effective way to deal with those who still doubt their eternal life, after they seemingly understand the gospel, is to go over one or two verses, perhaps John 6:37 and 39, and lovingly and firmly keep going over them until the person really believes what God is saying.

MEMORY VERSES FOR CHAPTER TWO

* John 6:37, 39
* I Peter 1:4,5
I Corinthians 6: 19
Ephesians 1: 13, 14
John 14:16, 17
* John 10:28
* Hebrews 10:10, 14
* John 5:24
Colossians 2: 13
* Acts 13:39
Romans 8:38, 39
* I John 5:10-13
Numbers 23:19

NOTE: If you are unaccustomed to memorizing Scripture, we recommend you start with the verses marked*.

CHAPTER III—CHASTENING AND REWARDS

Yes! Eternal life is guaranteed to all believers, but never make the mistake of thinking Christians can live as they please. They cannot. They can try, but God will not allow it. This should be made very clear as you witness. This is very important because failure to make this clear can keep a person from wanting to trust Christ as his Saviour.

When you are saved, you become God's son, and while you have certain privileges as God's child, remember that God is now your Father and has the responsibility of taking care of you. If a person thinks a Christian could live in sin and not be punished for it, he doesn't know much of the Bible, nor does he understand the working of the Holy Spirit in the life of a Christian.

History attests to the fact that when evil is allowed to go unpunished, it multiplies and causes heartbreaking damage. Confucius created a social situation that amazed the world: Under his system there was no crime problem. Why? He punished evil and rewarded good. Confucius followed the same plan God uses in dealing with His children.

God deals with His children mainly in two ways: (1) When you respond to and obey the Lord's leading in your life, God's discipline for you will be mainly one of guidance, encouragement, and further instruction; (2) When you rebel against God's leading, He will deal with you in however strong a measure it takes for you to obey Him. People are motivated mainly by two things: love and fear. God uses each in a perfect blend that is just right for each Christian.

Proverbs 3:11, 12, "My son, despise not the chastening of the Lord; neither be weary of His correction: For whom the Lord LOVETH He correcteth; even as a father the son in whom he delighteth." This is quoted in Heb. 12:6. Notice, when God corrects you, is it because He hates you? No, but because He loves you and knows what is best for you.

Job 5:17, "Behold, happy is the man whom God correcteth: therefore despise not thou the chastening of the Almighty."

When a Christian disobeys God, he should confess it right away. "If we confess our sins, He is faithful and just to for give us our sins, and to cleanse us from all unrighteousness" (I John 1:9). Every time you sin, you should confess it. Every time you confess your sin, you will be forgiven.

Please notice two other things about I John 1:9:.

(1) God does not guarantee restoration of fellowship on the basis of confession of sin. Fellowship with the Lord comes when a Christian disciplines his life so that he has "things in common" with the Lord.

(2) God does not guarantee restoration of damage resulting from sin on the basis of confession of sin. For instance, perhaps a Christian has gone away from things of the Lord and starts to drink, and he ruins his kidneys. If he confesses his sin, yes, the Lord will forgive him... but that forgiveness doesn't heal his damaged kidneys.

There is a natural result of sin as well as God's personal chastisement in your life. Galatians 6:7 says, "Be not deceived; God is not mocked; for whatsoever a man soweth, that shall he also reap." Notice that God does NOT add, "EXCEPT if he confesses it."

A Christian can do wrong things, but he cannot escape the CONSEQUENCES of doing wrong things. A person can put his hand into the fire if he wants to, but he cannot escape getting his hand burned. Some Christians want to sow wild oats all week long and then pray for CROP FAILURE at the end of the week!

One could not say how often you could commit the same sin before God would severely chasten you for it. The Lord uses His discretion in every instance. You will receive "personalized" attention. People often want to know "what God will do to them" if they do "thus and so." Hebrews 12:11 says when God chastens you it will not be pleasant: "Now no chastening for the present seemeth to be joyous, but grievous: nevertheless afterward it yieldeth the peaceable fruit of righteousness unto them which are exercised thereby."

A disobedient child is never happy. Continued sin often brings weakness and sickness into your life. If you refuse to respond to God's dealings with you, if you refuse to discipline your life, God can even take you home earlier than He would have otherwise

(I Cor. 11:30-32).

An example of a Christian taken home by God before his time because of sin is found in I Cor. 5:1-5. This person was committing adultery with his mother (or stepmother). Verse five says this person's body was destroyed-he was taken home-but please notice that he did not lose his salvation. In I Cor. 3:15 we read, "If any man's work shall be burned, he shall suffer loss: but he himself shall be saved...." Sin in the life of a Christian will result in a loss of his joy, power, testimony, fellowship, and reward.

The passage of Scripture, I Cor. 3:11-15, should be clearly understood by the soulwinner because it gives a good picture of what happens at the Judgment Seat of Christ for believers, and understanding this subject thoroughly will better enable you to answer questions that the lost often ask, such as: "How could God be just and fair if He lets both good people and bad people into heaven?"

Even though everyone is a sinner, and even though Christ has given complete forgiveness of all sin to all those who receive Him as Saviour, yet God still has many ways of seeing that those who truly serve Him are rewarded, and those who do not serve Him suffer loss of reward both on earth and later in heaven.

Notice, in I Cor. 3:11, that the only foundation God recognizes is the foundation of Jesus Christ. Then, in v. 12, the Christian may build either good or bad works in his life once he is saved. In v. 13 we find that God will judge every person's work to see what was good and what was bad. Verse 14 says that those who have done good work will receive reward, but v. 15 clearly teaches that those who have not done good works will suffer loss of reward even though they will not lose their salvation.

Ephesians 2:8, 9 tells us we are saved by grace through faith, but verse ten says, "For we are His workmanship, created in Christ Jesus unto good works, which God hath before ordained that we should walk in them." God wants His children to live a life of service to Him-not to be saved, but because they are saved.

After a person trusts Christ for salvation he should heed Romans 12:1, 2 for service, "I beseech you therefore, brethren, by the mercies of God, that ye present your bodies a living sacrifice, holy, acceptable unto God, which is your reasonable service. And be not conformed to this world; but be ye transformed by the renewing of your mind, that ye may prove what is that good, and acceptable, and perfect will of God."

A life of service for the Lord will be richly rewarded both now and later. When you obey God's Word and let the Lord run your life, you will have love, joy, and peace in your life (Gal. 5:22). God promises, "If they obey and serve Him they shall spend their days in prosperity and their years in pleasures" (Job 36:11). Jesus said, "... I am come that they might have life, and that they might have it more abundantly" (John 10:10).

If you want God to honor your life, you must serve Him. And if you DO serve the Lord, God IS BOUND to honor your life. "... If any man serve Me, him will My Father honor" (John 12:26). The "secret" of "Christian Victory" is no more or less than obeying God. You might sometimes think disciplining your life to serve the Lord is difficult. What you want to do will often be the opposite of what God wants you to do, but the reward is great... and have you considered what it will cost you if you do not serve the Lord?

Job exhorts, "... who hath hardened himself against Him, and hath prospered?" (Job 9.4) Listen to the warning in Deut. 28:47, 48, "Because thou servedest not the Lord thy God with joyfulness, and with gladness of heart, for the abundance of all things; therefore shalt thou serve thine enemies which the Lord shall send against thee, in hunger, and in thirst, and in nakedness, and IN WANT OF ALL THINGS: and he shall put a yoke of iron upon thy neck until he have destroyed thee."

In Isaiah 30:1 God says those Christians who rebel against Him will have trouble... those who refuse the counsel of God in the Scriptures so that they can live their own lives of sin can expect trouble. "Woe to the rebellious children, saith the Lord, that take counsel, but not of Me; and that cover with a covering, but not of My spirit, that they may add sin to sin."

Satan will always give you the best excuses why you shouldn't obey God. But the decision as to what you will do with your life is completely up to you. As we have mentioned before, salvation is voluntary, and service is voluntary. If you do not serve the Lord, you will have no one to blame but yourself.

Perhaps you may feel you have no particular "talent" to give to the Lord. God says the greatest ABILITY in Christian work is DEPENDability. "... It is required in stewards that a man be found FAITHFUL" (I Cor. 4:2). It is not required that you are (1) popular, (2) wealthy, (3) successful, (4) educated, or (5) influential. God honors the believer who faithfully does his best for the Lord each day.

Notice in I Tim. 1:12 the reason that God put Paul into the ministry. It wasn't that God just "chose" him for some intangible, vague reason. Paul had proven to be a faithful servant already, and God put him into the ministry because he could be counted upon to continue being FAITHFUL.

An interesting insight God has given us into the real reasons why many people do wrong and think they can actually get away with it, even in the sight of God, is found in Ecclesiastes 8:11, "Because sentence against an evil work is not executed speedily, therefore the heart of the sons of men is fully set in them to do evil." People forget that there is usually a TIME LAPSE between planting and reaping. The result of what we do is often not produced until later. (But then, when we realize the harm that has been done, it is too late to remedy the damage.) Deut. 32:35 says, "To Me belongeth vengeance, and recompense; their foot shall slide in DUE TIME...."

What you plant in your life will always come up. If you sow to the flesh, you will have nothing but heartache. Worldly pleasures are (1) trouble to get, (2) they don't satisfy when you do get them, and (3) there is great sorrow when they are lost. It has been said that the life of the world is the "life of the constantly bursting bubble."

A disciplined life for the Lord will cost you work, time, and effort. But an undisciplined life costs much more. Usually you will find it is not so much a question of KNOWING God's will for your life as being willing to DO it.

Determine that your life is going to amount to something for the Lord, and then discipline your life to that end. Every successful business has a time-table... a plan of progress... a projection for the future. There is no room in today's world for the mediocre person. AIM FOR THE HIGHEST. Don't settle for being an "average Christian." After all, "average" is just as close to the bottom as it is to the top. Don't be ordinary. STAND UP for the Lord Jesus Christ, and serve Him with all that is within you.

Remember that happiness is not found in pleasure, money, laughter, fame, or getting what you think you want... but is a by-product of a Spirit-controlled, useful life for the Lord Jesus Christ. Your future is being determined by what you do TODAY. If you want to accomplish great things for the Lord in the future, you must accomplish something for the Lord today.

Even unsaved ministers, doctors, and psychiatrists know the best advice they could give a depressed and unhappy person is to help someone else-to go and be of service. This brings joy. The Lord, our Great Physician, knows that serving Him brings the highest joy possible. Instead of trying to "buck" God's plan, why not follow His advice and share in all the good things God wants to bring into your life?

God is looking all over this earth for those who are singlemindedly, sincerely wanting to serve Him, that He might exercise His mighty power in their lives. "For the eyes of the Lord run to and fro throughout the whole earth, to shew Himself strong in the behalf of them whose heart is perfect toward Him..." (II Chron. 16:9). God WANTS to do things for His children... but He cannot reward EVIL. When you serve Him, He will do all things for you.

Besides the contentment you will have now, as you live your life for the Lord, knowing you are truly experiencing the fullest life possible on this earth—that of being in the service of our King-our wonderful God also promises that the person who is a faithful servant here will be greatly rewarded in the kingdom of God.

While it would be wrong for the Christian to serve the Lord ONLY because he will be rewarded for it, there is nothing wrong with realizing that God has set such a HIGH VALUE upon serving Him that He does promise to reward His servants... and with living our lives in accordance with the standards of value that He has placed upon things.

In Hebrews 11:24-26 we find that Moses did just this. "By faith Moses, when he was come to years, refused to be called the son of Pharaoh's daughter; Choosing rather to suffer affliction with the people of God, than to enjoy the pleasures of sin for a season; Esteeming the reproach of Christ GREATER RICHES than the treasures in Egypt; for he had respect unto the recompense OF THE REWARD.?' Moses served the Lord, motivated by the knowledge of future reward.

"For the Son of man shall come in the glory of His Father with His angels, and then He shall reward every man according to his works." (Matt. 16:27). "His lord said unto him, Well done, thou good and faithful servant: thou hast been faithful over a few things, I will make thee ruler over many things: enter thou into the joy of thy lord" (Matt. 25:21).

"For we must all appear before the judgment seat of Christ; that every one may receive the things done in his body, according to that he hath done, whether it be good or bad" (II Cor. 5:10).

Make it very clear that this person is not in a judgment to determine if he will go to heaven or hell. That was determined while the person was still living on earth, on the basis of whether or not he had received Christ as his Saviour. But this is a judgment for believers only, to determine whether or not they will have rewards during the thousand-year reign of Christ on earth.

A person must build upon the foundation of the Lord Jesus Christ (I Cor. 3:11). Even the best works a person could build outside of Christ are only "filthy rags" and could never amount to the righteousness needed for eternal life in heaven (with or without rewards).

This must constantly be emphasized to people, and especially to an audience. If you are in the position of teaching a group on this subject, you must not only make the gospel clear in their minds, but clear enough in their minds so that they know how to make it clear to someone else; and not only so, but clear enough in the minds of your group so that they not only CAN make it clear to someone else, but that they will see the IMPORTANCE of staying with the gospel to others, until it is clear to them also.

Paul was expressing this in II Timothy 2:2 when he said, "And the things that thou has heard of me among many witnesses, the same commit thou to faithful men, who shall be able to teach others also."

We should serve the Lord for the praise of God and not for the praise of men. It is the Lord who will reward you. Certainly men will not. "Knowing that whatsoever good thing any man doeth, the same shall he receive OF THE LORD, whether he be bond or free" (Eph. 6:8).

Situations are bound to occur in your Christian service in which you have done something for the Lord but another Christian seems to be receiving all the credit. Don't let it bother you. The Lord is keeping the books. YOU will be rewarded for what YOU do regardless of how people look at it on earth. "Now he that planteth and he that watereth are one: and every man shall receive his OWN reward ACCORDING TO HIS OWN LABOUR" (I Cor. 3:8). "Therefore, my beloved brethren, be ye steadfast, unmoveable, always abounding in the work of the Lord, forasmuch as ye know that your labour is not in vain in the Lord" (I Cor. 15:58).

Instructions for a New Christian

Study Your Bible

"As newborn babes, desire the sincere milk of the Word, that ye may grow thereby" (I Peter 2:2).

A person has faith that Christ will save him when he hears the plan of salvation from the Word of God and believes it (John 5:24)... and a person strengthens his faith that the Lord will lead him in his Christian life as he studies God's Word, believes God's Word, and obeys God's Word. "So then faith cometh by hearing, and hearing by the Word of God" (Rom. 10:17).

The only way really to understand the Bible is to study it, and every Christian who studies his Bible will tell of the great enjoyment he has in doing so, as well as gaining much knowledge. God's Word is power! KNOWLEDGE of God's Word and HOW TO PRESENT His Word will give you the power necessary to be an effective soulwinner.

The Bible tells us to "Study to shew thyself approved unto God, a workman that needeth not to be ashamed, rightly dividing the Word of truth" (II Timothy 2:15).

Another reason why we should study the Bible is also found in II Timothy, chapter 3, v. 16, 17, "All Scripture is given by inspiration of God, and is PROFITABLE for doctrine, for reproof, for correction, for instruction in righteousness; That the man of God may be perfect, throughly furnished unto all good works." Encourage the new believer to read his Bible, perhaps beginning with the Gospel of St. John.

Pray

Prayer is not some stilted, memorized speech that you make to God but conversation with your heavenly Father, who loves you very much. It should be just as natural for a Christian to talk to the Lord as it is for a little boy to talk to his Daddy. In fact, in Romans 8:15 the word "Abba," referring to our heavenly Father, is actually a very close, personal term, just like our word "Daddy" is today. Children of God can know Him intimately. There is no reason why a Christian should approach God in prayer with formal speeches. It does not show disrespect for God to address Him personally, but rather, it shows Him that we love Him deeply. Galatians 4:6 says that God Himself has sent forth the Spirit of His Son into our hearts, so that we would call our Father "Abba." God really wants us to "feel at home" when we talk things over with Him.

God invites us to talk to Him, "Call unto Me, and I will answer thee, and shew thee great and mighty things, which thou knowest not" (Jer. 3:3).

One of the wonderful things about prayer is that the Lord will never turn a deaf ear to you: He is always interested in what affects you. I Peter 5:7, "Casting all your care upon Him; for He careth for you." Encourage the new believer to pray often every day.

Meet Together With Other Christians

Your love for the Lord, for Christians, and for the unsaved will be greatly increased as you meet with believers and have fellowship with them. The New Testament believers gathered together often for prayer, Bible study, and to encourage one another in their witnessing and comfort one another in their testings.

"And when they were come, and had gathered the church together, they rehearsed all that God had done with them..." (Acts 14:27).

"Not forsaking the assembling of ourselves together, as the manner of some is; but exhorting one another: and so much the more, as ye see the day approaching" (Heb.10:25).

Also see Acts 15:4; Acts 20:7; Acts 21:18-20; and Galatians 6:1, 2.

It is the rare person who can withstand the pressures of his friends. If your friends are not those who know the Lord and take a stand in serving Him, they will constantly pull you down. It is of utmost importance to make your friends the kind of Christian you aspire to be.

Some of the most precious times in the lives of Christians have been spent in the prayer meetings of churches where believers gathered together to share their needs and help one another through the encouragement of testimonies and the power of earnest, intercessory prayer. Encourage the new believer to attend a good, Bible-believing and teaching church.

Tell Others How To Be Saved

A person who has just trusted Christ is often radiantly happy about experiencing the love of God. This glowing "first love" is best nurtured by telling others that God also loves them, and explaining how they, too, can be saved. A newly-saved person usually will readily see the need for his friends to trust Christ as their Saviour and will be eager to witness.

While endless preparation can go into learning how to witness most effectively, never leave a new Christian thinking witnessing should be done only by pastors and Bible college graduates. It is the responsibility of every Christian.

"But as we were allowed of God to be put in trust with the gospel, even so we speak, not as pleasing men, but God, which trieth our hearts" (I Thess. 2:4).

It is such a privilege for us... that God would actually put US in trust with His wonderful gospel message! It is not only a privilege in the sense that we can exercise it or not at our own choosing, but once we have the Holy Spirit living in us (as all Christians do), He works in us and gives us a desire to witness for Him that is all but impossible to ignore.

"Then I said, I will not make mention of Him, not speak any more in His Name. But His Word was in mine heart as a burning fire shut up in my bones, and I was weary with forbearing, and I COULD NOT STAY" (Jeremiah 20:9).

God says that all those who have been reconciled to Him -those who have been given a righteousness through trusting Christ as their Saviour-are His AMBASSADORS.

"And all things are of God, who hath reconciled us to Himself by Jesus Christ, and hath given to US the ministry of reconciliation; To wit, that God was in Christ, reconciling the world unto Himself, not imputing their trespasses unto them; and hath committed unto US the word of reconciliation. Now then WE ARE AMBASSADORS FOR CHRIST, as though God did beseech you by us: we pray you in Christ's stead, be ye reconciled to God" (II Cor. 5:18-20).

Any person who understands enough of the plan of salvation to receive Christ as his Saviour knows enough to tell others what happened to him and how they also may be saved. Often, even after you know the Bible very well, the most effective witness you could give would be your own testimony with a few, simple, salvation verses. Encourage the new believer to be a witness for the Lord.

Give the new Christian some literature that is clear on salvation. Chapter 22 of this book recommends literature of interest to the soulwinner and to the new Christian as well. A very effective tract, which has a distribution of over three million, "Am I Going to Heaven?" is pictured in Chapter Five. This tract is about salvation and is very good to leave with a new Christian.

The Holy Spirit indwells every believer and will guide the Christian in all facets of his life in Christ. Your example and testimony before the new Christian, as the one who led him to the Lord, will no doubt influence him very greatly, especially at first. As you pray for him, pray also for your self, that you will always be the proper influence.

As you see your child in the faith endeavoring to serve the Lord, you should encourage him to be water baptized as a testimony to others that not only is he saved, but also he now wants the Lord to use his life for His glory (Romans 6:4). (See Chapter Nine for coverage of the false teaching that man must be water baptized for salvation.)

MEMORY VERSES FOR CHAPTER THREE

Proverbs 3:11, 12

* 1 John 1: 9
* I Corinthians 5:5
* I Corinthians 3:15
* I Corinthians 11:30
* Ephesians 2:10
* Romans 12:1, 2
* Galatians 5:22, 23
Job 36:11
* I Corinthians 4:2
* II Corinthians 5:10
* I Corinthians 3:11
I Corinthians 15:58
I Corinthians 3:8
I Peter 2:2
* Romans 10:17
I Peter 5:7
Hebrews 10:25
* Hebrews 12:6, 11
* I Thessalonians 2:4

CHAPTER IV—THE MESSENGER
YOUR TESTIMONY

"This is a faithful saying, and these things I will that thou affirm constantly, that they which have believed in God might be careful to maintain good works. These things are good and profitable unto men" Titus 3:8).

The Bible says to BE CAREFUL to maintain good works. You can be sure that Satan will "pull every trick" to get you to ruin your testimony. Scripture says, "Be sober, be vigilant, because your adversary, the devil, as a roaring lion, walketh about, seeking whom he may DEVOUR" (I Pet. 5:8).

You will have to "Put on the whole armour of God, that ye may be able to stand against the wiles of the devil" (Eph. 6: 11).

Many times when a Christian is sound doctrinally and determined to witness, Satan will "sneak around the back door" and ruin that Christian's effectiveness because he wasn't CAREFUL in his testimony.

This is so important! God warns us, "Giving no offense in any thing, that the MINISTRY be not blamed!" (II Cor. 6:3) We should do what is proper in every situation because people will use our poor testimony to criticize Christian work.

If people find that you lie, cheat, steal, speak in an uncouth manner, gossip, are inconsiderate of others, etc., you will not be liked, and you will do GREAT HARM to your ministry. People will look at your life and say, "If that is an example of Christianity, then I don't want it."

The Lord cautions us to "Abstain from all appearance of evil" (I Thess. 5:22). Some things might be perfectly harmless for you to do, not sinful to you in any way, except that some Christians would consider it a poor testimony for one reason or another. God says, in that case, to abstain from it. Just don't do it. It isn't worth it. Your ministry-what you are trying to accomplish in your life for the Lord-is too valuable for you to risk its losing any effectiveness. God knows your heart, and He will bless you for your faithfulness.

The Apostle Paul was in a situation similar to this. In his day it was common for meat which had been offered to idols afterwards to be placed in the market for sale. He knew the meat was neither blessed nor cursed by the idol (I Cor. 8:8). But there were Christians who thought Paul should not eat that meat.

Could Paul have eaten the meat? Yes. Did he? No! Why? He said, "It is good neither to eat flesh, nor to drink wine, nor anything whereby thy brother stumbleth, or is offended, or is made weak" (Rom. 14:21). "Wherefore, if meat make my brother to offend, I will eat no flesh while the world standeth, lest I make my brother to offend" (I Cor. 8:13). In Christian work you cannot offend people... and neither can you let yourself be offended. If you allow people to hurt your feelings, you will not be able to have the ministry with them in their lives that you need to have.

PAUL DISCIPLINED HIS OWN LIFE IN ORDER TO SERVE AND HELP OTHERS.

As a soulwinner, you will probably "give up" things that the average Christian wouldn't even question-not because you have to-but because you love the Lord so much that you wouldn't want anything in your life to keep people from trusting Christ as their Saviour.

"All things are lawful unto me, but all things are not expedient: all things are lawful for me, but I will not be brought under the power of any" (I Cor. 6:12).

It is not a question of "Can you do this or that and still be saved?" And it wasn't that question in Paul's case. He knew the law could not affect his eternal life. But he kept himself from becoming enslaved by sin in his daily life (Rom. 6:15, 16) so he could be more greatly used for the Lord.

"For brethren, ye have been called unto liberty; only use not liberty for an occasion to the flesh, but by love serve one another" (Gal. 5:13).

To be a fruitful witness for the Lord you must voluntarily discipline your life to carry the correct testimony for your Lord and Saviour. If you tell people about Christ and don't honor Christ in your life, people won't respect you and will not listen when you witness.

However, don't go to the opposite extreme either. Some Christians get so introspective that they spend all their time trying to be "holy," spend hours in "prayer and meditation," but neglect to tell the lost about Christ. They live "good lives" before others, but no one ever hears the gospel from their lips. If you live a good life but don't witness, you will get all the glory instead of Christ, to whom all glory belongs (I Cor. 1:31).

It is amazing what high standards even the world sets for Christians, and truly we should live the best possible life and testimony. You will be labeled as a "fanatic" if you witness without a life to back it up. A good testimony and a good witness go hand-in-hand. You must have both really to glorify the Lord. They are not in competition.

Satan will deceive anyone who will accept his "line," whether that person be saved or unsaved. John 8:44 says Satan is a liar and the father of lies. Satan tries to get the lost to live good lives, deceiving them that this would help them get to heaven. Satan tries to keep the saved from living good lives, because he knows that this will keep the lost from accepting the gospel when it is presented.

I Thessalonians, chapter two, mentions many qualities Paul had as a soulwinner. As you study this passage, you will notice that he (1) was bold in his witness, (2) used no deceit or trickery, (3) fulfilled his trust and pleased God, (4) was honest, (5) didn't seek the praise of men, (6) was gentle, (7) had great love and concern, (8) labored diligently, (9) carried a good testimony, and (10) taught them to live for the Lord.

If you want to be a great soulwinner, you must be a great servant. "... whosoever will be great among you, shall be your MINISTER" (Mark 10:43).

The Apostle Paul is a wonderful example of a really dedicated Christian. Listen to his own words in I Cor. 9:1 and 19. "Am I not an apostle? Am I not free? Have I not seen Jesus Christ our Lord? Are not ye my work in the Lord? For though I be free from all men, yet have I made myself servant unto all, that I might gain the more."

Do you realize the extent of the dedication of the Apostle Paul? Yes, he witnessed night and day for three years straight, publicly and privately (Acts 20:20, 21, 31). But what was he willing to give up to lead a soul to Christ?

MONEY? POSITION? SPARE TIME? SPORTS? HOME? HEALTH? LIFE ITSELF?

Did you know that he was willing to have given his OWN SOUL that others could be saved? I Thess. 2:8 tells us, "So being affectionately desirous of you, we were willing to have imparted unto you, not the gospel of God only, but also OUR OWN SOULS, because ye were dear unto us." Paul cared so much for souls that he was willing, if it were possible even to go to hell himself, if that would help his fellow Jews to be saved (Romans 9:3).

Some things aren't even a poor testimony in themselves, but they "bog" you down, they are "weights," they take up valuable time which you should be using for the Lord. Hebrews 12:1 says to "lay aside every weight."

Your life can become filled with so many "good" things of this life that you haven't the time to do much for Christ. If you really want to join in this battle for souls, heed the Scripture which says, "No man that warreth entangles himself with the affairs of this life, that he may please Him who hath chosen him to be a soldier" (II Tim. 2:4).

No one can tell you how to run your life... what to include in your schedule, and what to leave out. You could probably rationalize and excuse any activity which you wanted to. But between you and the Lord you must decide what is best for your service to Him.

Your time is your life. You do not know how much you have. How you spend your time each day will determine the total worth of your life. Your future is being determined by what you do each day. If your life is made up largely of sports, money, pleasure, television, clubs, etc., then your life will come and go-and not much will be accomplished for Christ in it.

Paul said that for him to live was "Christ." He spent his time on things that were valuable to Christ. How do you spend your time? Mostly on yourself, or mostly for Christ? Can you say, "For to me to live is Christ, and to die is gain"? (Phil. 1:21) If your time is spent for Christ, dying truly will be gain for you, for you will have much reward in heaven.

YOUR BIBLE

God says in II Tim. 3: 15, "... the holy Scriptures... are able to make thee wise unto salvation through faith which is in Christ Jesus." "So then faith cometh by hearing, and hearing by the Word of God" (Rom. 10:17).

God exalts His Word even above His own Name (Psalm 138:2). With such high recommendation from God Himself, we certainly should know the Bible WELL, for our own personal comfort and exhortation and to bring the gospel message to the lost.

In many parts of the world today the governments will not allow Bibles to be printed, and Bibles have to be smuggled into the country. If there is one printed copy of the Word of God in the entire congregation, the people consider themselves fortunate... and this one Bible is passed from family to family, who eagerly copy portions by hand, so that they may have some of the precious Word of God written down for use in their homes. Today in America we sometimes don't stop to realize how fortunate we are with our open Bibles.

The familiar verse, II Tim. 2:15, "Study to shew thyself approved unto God, a workman that needeth not to be ashamed, rightly dividing the Word of truth" should be taken very seriously.

Yes, it is possible to win souls with very little knowledge of Scripture. A baby is not expected to have the knowledge of a college graduate. But when a baby remains infantile all his life, it is certainly a great tragedy.

God says, "As newborn babes, desire the sincere milk of the Word, that ye may GROW thereby" (I Peter 2:2). Those who desire to be FRUITFUL soulwinners should be "ready always to give an answer to every man that asketh (him) a reason of the hope that is in (him)..." (I Pet. 3: 15).

Paul said he was "... READY to preach the gospel..." (Rom. 1:15). To be ready to preach the gospel in such a way that will answer people's questions will require that you spend time MEMORIZING Scriptures on salvation and studying thoroughly the passages which answer people's questions.

GOD'S WORD IS POWER! Knowledge of God's Word and how to best present it is your greatest "weapon" in witnessing. "For the Word of God is quick, and powerful, and sharper than any twoedged sword, piercing even to the dividing asunder of soul and spirit, and of the joints and marrow, and is a discerner of the thoughts and intents of the heart" (Hebrews 4:12).

Even when you are talking to someone who says he doesn't believe the Bible, don't stop using it. A soldier doesn't throw down his sword just because the opposition doesn't think it will work. The lost will never see salvation without the Word of God. It is the entrance of God's Word that gives light to the lost (Psalm 119:130).

Yes, there are times when a person needs a lengthy explanation of something, and you will need more than a verse of Scripture to adequately answer his question. But be watchful that you don't embark upon a philosophical discussion of no profit to the man's salvation.

The Apostle Paul was highly educated by the finest instructors of his day, and yet he said of his witnessing, "My speech and my preaching was not with enticing words of MAN'S wisdom, but in demonstration of the Spirit and of power: that your faith should not stand in the wisdom of men, but in the power of GOD" (I Cor. 2:4, 5).

Paul was concerned that his children in the faith might not always keep their message simple and Christ-centered, and warned them of Satan's tactics, "But I fear, lest by any

means, as the serpent beguiled Eve through his SUBTILTY, so your minds should be corrupted from the simplicity that is in Christ" (II Cor. 11:3).

Satan won't say to you, "Hello, this is Satan speaking, and if you just simply present the gospel, most people will accept it, but I want people to go to hell, so please complicate the gospel by using technical words, or having a philosophical discussion, or by adding man's good works and righteousness for salvation, so they won't receive Christ as their Saviour."

NOT AT ALL!

Satan comes in with a sweet, quiet voice and might say, "Look, Christian, this person is a very moral, intelligent, up-to-date citizen. If you start talking to him about the Bible, sin, Jesus' blood, and having faith, etc., he will think you are absolutely NUTS.

"So what you should do is to approach this person on an intellectual plane, so he will think you are educated and on his level. Tell him how good he is, how wonderful it is to be broadminded. Don't offend him by talking about the blood of Christ, but rather, discuss the love of God and the wonderful achievements of modern man and society today, and you could slowly turn his thoughts toward religion and a belief in God."

MANY people are fooled by this trickery of Satan. Don't fall for Satan's lie. DON'T BE FOOLED! Give out the gospel purely and simply.

USE THE SCRIPTURES!

Even some students in Bible college, who really love the Lord and His Word, are blinded by Satan into thinking they could effectively win souls through some "philosophical approach" rather than by using the Word of God, depending upon the Holy

Spirit. Paul also said, "Beware lest any man spoil you through philosophy and vain deceit, after the tradition of men, after the rudiments of the world, and NOT AFTER CHRIST" (Col. 2:8).

It cannot be emphasized too strongly that the GOSPEL is the power God uses to save people. Now I do not mean by this that you do not adapt your illustrations and examples to interest the particular person you are witnessing to. You should witness with his background in mind. For instance, you would use the scientific-statements in the Bible to interest a chemistry major in college, or astronomical or medical statements in the Bible with those interested in astronomy or medicine, etc.

Use the things in your own testimony that would establish rapport between you. For instance, when I talk to a Jewish person, I usually mention that I am part Jewish and attended synagogue for two years. When I talk to a Catholic, I might mention I took a six-month catechism course in a Roman Catholic church. When talking to a Protestant, I can mention that I spent three years attending different Protestant churches. All these things are true, and yet they would not all interest every person to the same degree. So I try to think in terms of the other person's background and establish some common ground between us.

This does not mean a compromise on DOCTRINE, but it allows me to have an empathy established, which is very helpful in witnessing. Think back upon your own life and you will be amazed to discover what interesting things have happened to you (they MUST be true) that you can profitably use in witnessing. And then, DO use them. People are usually interested in what has happened to someone else. It doesn't seem to put THEM on the "spot." This helped Paul's witnessing, too (I Cor. 9:19-23).

But it is the SCRIPTURES, it is the GOSPEL that will save-not your wisdom. Because of man's natural pride, it will be very easy to fall into this snare of Satan's of using too much of your own philosophy and not enough of the Word of God.

How To Study Your Bible

If at all possible, it is wise to set aside a special time for your Bible study and not to let Satan sidetrack you to do something else during that time. You will never "find" time to study, pray, or witness-you must "make" time. People usually manage to have time for whatever is really important to them. To study your Bible so that you have a thorough working knowledge of it is important to you as a soulwinner for many reasons:

(1) It is God's command to you (II Tim. 2:15).
(2) God's Word brings faith (Rom. 10:17).
    It will not only bring to the lost the knowledge of salvation, but it will also strengthen your own faith.
(3) You will use the Word to edify, exhort, guide, and comfort Christians under your care (II Tim. 4:2).
(4) The Bible is your own guidebook for every situation of life, and you will want to have what God says at your "fingertips" (Matt. 4:4).
(5) The Word of God is part of your defensive weapon against Satan's attacks upon you (Eph. 6:17). Remember how Christ rebuked Satan by using Scripture (Matt. 4:10, 11).

Below are some hints toward successful Bible study.

A. Read with the INTENTION OF REMEMBERING what you read.
B. GO OVER what you have read until it is clear in your mind.
C. MAKE NOTES on the things that impress you as you read.
D. COMPARE SCRIPTURE WITH SCRIPTURE to understand the passage in its proper relationship with the rest of the Word of God.
E. ANALYZE the verse:
   1) Who wrote it?
   2) To whom was it written?
   3) What general topic is being discussed? (Consider the context.)
   4) What does it NOT say?
   5) What things COULD it mean?
   6) Eliminate the possible meanings by comparing it with other Scripture until you feel you have the right one.
F. If you still do not understand a passage:

1) LOOK UP WORDS which are unclear to you in a concordance. A good one is Strong's Concordance, published by Abingdon Press, which lists every word in the English Bible and gives the Hebrew or Greek word and its translation. It is the work of over one hundred scholars.
   2) LOOK UP THE PASSAGE in other good translations of the Bible. Some are:
   American Standard
   Williams
   Amplified
   3) STUDY the passage with the help of GOOD COMMENTARIES. Some are:
   DeHann
   H. A. Ironside
   G. Campbell Morgan
   C. H. Spurgeon
   Woodbridge
   4) Discuss the passage with another Christian and get his viewpoint of the Scripture.
G. KEEP A NOTEBOOK. When you are satisfied with a particular explanation, write down your conclusion and file it under a topical heading. After a while you will have collected much good information that will help you greatly in your private study and public teaching ministry in the future.
H. REFERENCE YOUR BIBLE. When a verse stands out in your mind as the key verse on a given subject, use that verse as a place to list the references of other verses on that subject in the margin right beside it.
I. SELECT A BIBLE WITH CLEAR PRINT. We like the Scofield Reference Bible, which is a King James translation and has notes and references which are very helpful in study. Get the Bible with the best cover and paper that you can afford because it will last the longest.
Treat your Bible with care. When a cover becomes too shabby, you might want to have it rebound rather than to transfer your notes into a new Bible. If you do get a new Bible, try to get the same kind where the same passage is found on the same place on the page. This is good because much of your memory is "sight-oriented." You will automatically find yourself looking for the verse where you are accustomed to seeing it on the page.
J. As you study, memorize the plan of salvation in a brief outline form, maybe just seven points... for instance:
   1) All sinners-Rom. 3:23
   2) Result-death-Rom. 6:23
   3) Heaven perfect-Rev. 21:27
   4) Cannot earn-Eph. 2:8, 9
   5) Christ paid and gives righteousness-II Cor. 5:21; Phil. 3:9
   6) Only believe-John 3:16
   7) Know you have eternal life-I John 5:13

This will be extremely valuable when you witness... not that you will quote it verbatim as you witness... but your mind will then be free to start right in with the gospel even when you are nervous and may perhaps otherwise be caught tongue-tied for lack of knowing what to say.

Memorizing the main points of what one wants to cover has been a successful procedure in business where person-to-person contact is required in any type of sales or persuasion. The soulwinner should use any Scriptural methods and techniques that work as an aid in his witnessing.

Your Love

In Romans 1:1 Paul says he is a "servant" of Jesus Christ. The Greek word for servant is "doulos" and means "slave." Paul served the Lord with a voluntary love. A person in love feels compelled to please the one he loves and yet is not forced to. No law says the young man must be courteous and kind to the girl he loves... he does not have to, but he finds he wants to. What girl would want flowers if the boy felt he had to bring them? What girl would want a gift of candy or perfume if her boy friend felt he was obliged to give her a present? When you are in love, you desire only voluntary expressions of it. Force would take away any meaning it might otherwise have had.

God did not choose to make us puppets that would act as He manipulated them, bowing when He pulled one string, speaking when He pulled another. Our loving God is the per-son who wanted us to have a great capacity to love-to love Him-and to love others... but love must be voluntary, or it isn't really love at all.

One of the many serious flaws of communism is that it can never bring satisfaction to its subjects because there is no place for love in its system. God created us with an enormous capacity and craving for love. No human being can completely fill the need of another for this love. One philosopher, Pascal, said well, "There is a God-shaped vacuum in every man, and only God can fill it."

It was verses like John 3:16, which tell of God's great love, that caused me to accept Christ as my Saviour. It does something to me when I realize that the God who made everything in the entire universe actually loves me. I do not understand how this could be, but I believe it and do so respond to His love that it has changed my whole life.

Something about my make-up causes me to want to please someone who really loves me. I cannot be indifferent to a person who loves me. Can you?

It is not always easy to analyze why we love someone, but when it comes to our love for the Lord, the reasons are abundant. A Christian cannot read his Bible for very long without finding so many characteristics of our Lord that just compel us to love Him more and more.

The more you serve the Lord, the more you "put on the line" for Him, the more your love for Him will grow. Many Christians express a desire to feel closer to the Lord. Reading His Word will help greatly, but one sure way is actually to get out and SERVE the Lord with your whole heart. Working "hand in hand" with the Lord forms a great bond of sweet and conscious fellowship that is very satisfying. I believe this is part of what the Apostle Paul was bringing out in Galatians 5:22, "The fruit of the Spirit is love, joy, peace.

..." The result of letting your life be controlled by the Spirit, obeying God's leading, really brings love into your life-love for the Lord... love for the lost... and love for Christians, too.

This love for the Lord is not some "gushy" love. It is a very practical love that causes Christians to do many things for the Lord, some of which can even be unpleasant things in themselves.

A mother who gets up in the middle of the night to take care of her sick child is not doing so because she just "loves" to lose sleep, and just "loves" to be around vomit... but because she has a real, deep LOVE and CONCERN for her child.

Can you imagine what Christian service would be like if God had kept us under law, and not under grace, for us to live by? Because we are saved as a gift of God's grace, we feel such an overwhelming debt of gratitude to the Lord that just anything we can do for Him is a real pleasure. How could we possibly begin to repay God for what He has done for us?

In Luke 7:47 Christ explains that one who has been forgiven of much sin will certainly love God much; haven't we, therefore, much capacity to love Him?

It is a very sad thing to hear of seemingly sincere members of various religions living lives of terrible, physical and mental torture, thinking this would somehow please God. If only they would believe God when He says over and over again in the Bible that He does NOT delight in our "sacrifices and offerings" for salvation, and that furthermore, it is the "love of Christ" that should constrain us to serve Him, not fear. Yes, fear will. But God would so much prefer that we serve Him because we love Him.

Stop and think...
God saved you by His grace,
God keeps you saved by His grace,
God leads and guides you by His grace,
God enables you to serve Him by His grace,
God rewards you with love, joy, and peace in this life for serving Him by His grace,
God rewards you in heaven for having served Him on earth... SUCH GRACE!

Surely, God is good, and with the Psalmist we must say, "What shall I render unto the Lord for all His benefits toward me?" (Psa. 116:12)

I love the Lord, don't you?

CHAPTER V—THE OPENING AND THE CLOSE

If you have contact with a person by mail, at the store, in a gas station, waiting for a bus, at church, or in your home, you have an opportunity to witness for Christ.

We believe it is a very rare instance when the Lord Himself would actually prefer that you say nothing at all about Him.

You perhaps will not have the opportunity to fully explain the plan of salvation to everyone with whom you have contact, but you should definitely be in prayer continually as to exactly what God WOULD have you say.

There could never be "rules" for conversation openers because each time you meet someone you will have to judge the situation. However, there are some guidelines which can help you as you are beginning to witness. In time you will discover which ways work best for you in certain situations, and you will usually be able to sense, through the leading of the Holy Spirit, the best way to approach the person with the gospel.

It is very important, as you begin to witness, to gain "favorable attention." Be friendly. Be pleasant. Be gracious. Look for opportunities to give a sincere compliment. Be alert to notice (from the other person's remarks) what his interests are, and what his philosophies are, so you can make use of these clues he has given you as you present the gospel to him. The wonderful thing about the gospel is that it meets the needs of every individual, but we should be careful to explain it properly to people so that they can SEE it will meet their need. Sometimes several approaches will be necessary before you discover what will really open the person up to the love of Christ. Perhaps this is the key thought-not the exact words you will say so much as how you can get the person's mind open to the Lord and the Bible.

If the Lord leads you to start witnessing "cold, right off the bat" to someone you have never met-fine. Do it. However, you will usually find the person more receptive to the gospel if you can first talk with him about something he is already interested in. Sometimes you will take as long as half an hour or more in doing this; other times you can do it in a very few minutes. Each person and situation will be different, and the Lord will lead you as you go about "preparing the way" for a good presentation of the gospel.

We are not suggesting you "beat around the bush" when you witness. Not at all. But you will find that if first you speak to the person in terms of what interests HIM, he will be more disposed to listen when you speak about what interests YOU.

Your interest in this person should be genuine. You will find that people are absolutely starving for someone to care about them. This is so MUCH to your advantage. The time and effort you spend being kind to the person will really pay off in souls won to Christ, and in your influence upon him to serve the Lord after he is saved, as well.

A careful reading of Dale Carnegie's book How to Win Friends and Influence People should be of great value to you as a soulwinner. This is not advocating trickery of any sort, nor is it minimizing the work of the Holy Spirit. But it is well to have a thorough understanding of what motivates people and to use this understanding correctly for the Lord Jesus Christ. The principles in Mr. Carnegie's book are generally quite Scriptural and are presented in a clear, interesting manner.

Below is a sample conversation I might use as I start witnessing to a saleslady. You can use this approach to people of all walks of life, asking them how they became interested in whatever line of work they happen to be in.

WITNESS: "How did you become interested in selling clothing?"

SALESLADY: "As a teenager I was interested in fashion, so I was happy to get this job a few years ago in women's apparel."

WITNESS: "Guess you meet all kinds of people in selling."

SALESLADY: "Yes, it is very interesting. What kind of work are you in?"

Note: People invariably ask what you do after you have spoken to them about what they do. No matter WHAT your vocation is, your answer can be used to lead them into the gospel.

WITNESS: "I am a pilot... but my main interest is in people."

Note: Here is where you can give your personal testimony. As you are reading this book, take time out and go over your testimony and think of things that would be of interest to most people. This doesn't mean to make up things and put them into your testimony. Some Christians lament that their testimony isn't "interesting." But you will be amazed, if you spend time thinking and planning, how many little things have occurred in your life that you can word in such a way as to be extremely interesting to others. Most people will be interested in hearing what has happened to you. There is a certain curiosity value here.

As you plan, you should arrange your testimony into various lengths of presentation. You should be able to give the plan of salvation through your testimony in two minutes, five minutes, ten minutes, half an hour, or hours. When you have this settled in your mind and ready for use as the situation indicates, you will find you have more courage to witness because you will be prepared.

You like to talk about what you know. A baseball enthusiast loves to talk about baseball and revels in his knowledge of the players' averages. I'm sure you know people who think they are experts in some subjects and can't wait for an opportunity to air their knowledge.

Fear or hesitancy to witness usually comes from a lack of confidence in your knowledge of the subject. Pat yourself on the back for being interested in studying soul winning enough to read this book! But, obviously, just reading a book cannot furnish you with all you need to win souls.

These four things will help you to overcome your fear of witnessing:

(1) Knowledge of the Scriptures,
(2) Successful past experiences,
(3) Being around people who also witness, and
(4) Prayer.

You will usually find that the fear you have of witnessing will disappear as soon as you actually begin to witness to the person. The important thing is to GET STARTED! Don't allow Satan to keep you from being an effective witness because of fear. Claim I John 4:18, "There is no fear in love: but perfect love casteth out fear: because fear hath torment. He that feareth is not made perfect in love." Remember, it is the "love of Christ that constrains" us to witness.

To be a great soulwinner, you must study and practice, study and practice, and study and practice some more. Another concrete aid in overcoming fear of witnessing is an "ever ready" presentation of the gospel through your own testimony.

If you have a close Christian friend who is also interested in soulwinning, perhaps you could get together and "practice" on each other. Give your testimony to each other as you would to a lost person. Hearing one another will help you in recognizing phrases you could word better, etc. Also, after you have given your testimony a few times, you will gain more confidence.

A tape recorder can also be helpful to you. Tape your testimony and see if you like how you sound. You might discover several things in your speaking you would like to change... perhaps you speak too fast, use too many "uh's," or repeat a favorite cliché more than is pleasing to the ear.

No one becomes a perfect soulwinner overnight. But remember, it isn't your eloquence, anyway, that God is going to bless, but your faithful, loving presentation of the gospel. The important thing is to START witnessing now. Witness to somebody TODAY. "He that goeth forth and weepeth, bearing precious seed, shall doubtless come again with rejoicing, bringing his sheaves with him" (Psalm 126:6).

USING CURRENT NEWS AS A CONVERSATION OPENER

If you can relate a current news item to Scripture as a fulfillment of prophecy, a conversation is then opened for the gospel.

The cancerous growth of socialism throughout the world, and this includes America, can be used to interest people in the Word of God. It probably is wise to leave "politics" as such out of the conversation, but at the same time there is no reason not to mention that government policies which aid atheism and socialism certainly are unscriptural.

There is an intricately involved study of prophetic Scripture on the subject of the "last world ruling power" which cannot be entered into in this handbook of personal evangelism, but we will mention some verses briefly you might want to use to arouse a person's interest in hearing more of the Bible-which, we pray, will be verses on salvation.

1. God foretells in Daniel 7:23 that the last world ruling power will "devour the whole earth." America is not excluded from this terrible dominion, as much as we wish it were.

2. Daniel 8:23 says the ruler of the latter time will use "dark sentences" which, according to the Hebrew, means "trickery."

3. Daniel 8:24 tells us of his great satanic power, the increase of his dominion, and the martyrdom of Christians at his hand.

4. Daniel 8: 25 lets us know that his policy is to use "craft." The Hebrew for this is "deceit." His policies shall be advanced through using deceit. He will think he is very great, but the Lord Jesus Christ, the Prince of princes, shall eventually conquer him.

5. Daniel 11:21 says this ruler shall say there will be peace (Hebrew, "promise of peace, false or true") and shall conquer nations through false platforms.

6. Daniel 11:24 This ruler shall have had no precedent in his wicked works. No man shall have done evil like this before. He will "scatter among them the prey"... promise great economic security to the nations, but not come through with his false promise except for a short time to gain their confidence and allegiance.

7. Daniel 11:36-The ruler will not believe in God. He will prosper until the end of the Great Tribulation when Christ shall break him in pieces (Dan. 2:45). Our beloved America is following this world-wide socialistic trend which we believe is the system God describes as the last world ruling power. The Ecumenical Movement also plays its part in this "one-worldism," which we shall discuss in Chapter 14.

When a person realizes that socialism is sweeping the entire world, including his own country, he is usually quite receptive to the gospel. Who would want to go through the Great Tribulation? God promises that His people will not have to. It is only for the unsaved on the earth at that time (1Thess. 1:10; 5:9; Rev. 3:10; Isa. 26:20).

It is not profitable to go into myriad detail on prophecy of this sort with a lost person because its proper understanding could not come until a person is saved and has studied the Bible quite thoroughly. But as a conversation opener-used to go from a general topic INTO THE GOSPEL-it can be very valuable.

USING PROPHECY OF THE JEWS AS A CONVERSATION OPENER

Hearing about something that has happened in our own lifetime impresses us more vividly than hearing of some thing that happened before we were born. For this reason, the return of the Jew to the land of Israel in May, 1948, is of particular value as a conversation opener. This prophecy was fulfilled within the lifetime of anyone over 46 years of age (as of this printing in 1994).

Amos 9:14, 15, "And I will bring again the captivity of My people of Israel, and they shall build the waste cities, and inhabit them; and they shall plant vineyards, and drink the wine thereof; they shall also make gardens, and eat the fruit of them. And I will plant them upon their land, and they shall no more be pulled up out of their land which I have given them, saith the Lord thy God."

Isaiah 27:12, "And it shall come to pass in that day, that the Lord shall beat off from the channel of the river unto the stream of Egypt, and ye shall be gathered one by one, O ye children of Israel."

Hosea 3:4, 5, "For the children of Israel shall abide many days without a king, and without a prince, and without a sacrifice, and without an image, and without an ephod, and without teraphim: Afterward shall the children of Israel return, and seek the Lord their God, and David their king; and shall fear the Lord and His goodness in the latter days. "

You might also mention WHY the Jews were scattered. In the twenty-sixth chapter of Leviticus God gives the conditions of blessings and warnings of chastisement for the nation Israel. The final chastisement after continued disobedience is DISPERSION.

Leviticus 26:32, 33, "And I will bring the land into desolation: and your enemies which dwell therein shall be astonished at it. And I will scatter you among the heathen, and will draw out a sword after you: and your land shall be desolate, and your cities waste."

Deuteronomy 28:63-66 describes the scope of the final Old Testament dispersion, "And it shall come to pass, that as the Lord rejoiced over you to do you good, and to multiply you; so the Lord will rejoice over you to destroy you, and to bring you to naught; and ye shall be plucked from off the land whither thou goest to possess it. And the Lord shall scatter thee among all people, from the one end of the earth even unto the other; and there thou shalt serve other gods, which neither thou nor thy fathers have known, even wood and stone."

In Mark 14:27 Christ quoted from Zechariah 13:7 which says, "... saith the Lord of hosts: smite the shepherd, and the sheep shall be scattered... ," indicating that the Jews would again be scattered, this time because of their attitude toward the Messiah- for not receiving Him.

If you will have in your mind what you want to say in regard to the Jews going back to the Land as a fulfilled prophecy, you will be amazed to discover how often the Lord will allow conversations of people around you to make a perfect gateway for your remarks.

This prophecy will arouse their interest in the Bible and you should then lead the conversation into the plan of salvation. Perhaps, if Jewish people are present, begin with prophecy about the Messiah. Chapter 12 of this book will give details on witnessing to Jews.

USING TRACTS TO OPEN CONVERSATIONS

AM I GOING TO HEAVEN?

Check What's Required:
1. Obeying God's law and commandments.
2. Gifts to charity.
3. Doing your best.
4. Living a good life.
5. Good works.
6. Trying to obey the Golden Rule.
7. Tithing, or giving money to the church.
8. Church membership.
9. Regular church attendance.
10. Prayers.
11. Fasting.
12. Water baptism.
13. Holy communion.
14. Born of Christian parents.
15. Confirmation.
16. Penances.
17. Extreme unction.

EXPLANATION:

No. 1—It is impossible to get to heaven this way. The Bible says: (see Romans 3:19-28).
"Therefore we conclude that a man is justified (vindicated) by faith without the deeds of the law." (Romans 3:28)

No. 2,3, or 4—These things could never save you. The Bible says:
"Not by works of righteousness which we have done, but according to His mercy He saved us..." (Titus 3:5)

No. 5,6, or 7—Good works can not save anyone. The Bible states:
"For by grace are you saved through faith; and that not of yourselves: It is the gift of God: Not of works, lest any man should boast." (Ephesians 2:8,9)

No. 8,9,10 or 11—We can not be saved by works, regardless of how good or well intended. God saves us by His grace (mercy). The Bible says: "And if by grace, then it is no more of works: otherwise grace is no more grace. but if it be of works, then is it no more grace: otherwise work is no more work." (Romans 11:6)

No. 12 or 13—Water baptism and communion are for those who are already saved. It is not our work that saves us, but faith in Christ. The Bible says:
"But to him that works not, but believes on Him that justifies the ungodly, his faith is counted for righteousness." (Romans 4:5)

No. 14—This can not save you. The Bible says:
"They which are the children of the flesh these are not the children of God..." (Romans 9:8)
"But as many as received Him (Christ), to them gave He power to become the Sons of God, even to them that believe on His Name: which were born, not of blood, nor of the will of the flesh, nor of the will of man, but of God." (John 1:12,13)
"Not of blood" means "not of one's parentage." You must be born of God to be saved.

No. 15,16 or 17—These are man-made doctrines and are not taught in the Bible. God says:
"But in vain they do worship Me, teaching for doctrines the commandments of men." (Matthew 15:9)

No! None of these things can save you. You can do nothing to earn eternal life. It is faith in the Lord Jesus Christ alone that can save you.

"And by Him (Christ) all that believe are justified from all things, from which you could not be justified by the law of Moses." (Acts 13:39)

The way to have eternal life is not found in what we do ourselves, but by having a perfect righteousness given to us. We receive this when we believe the Lord Jesus Christ took our sins on Himself and paid for them by His death on the cross.

"For He (God) has made Him (Christ) to be sin for us, who knew no sin; that we might be made the righteousness of God in Him." (II Corinthians 5:21)

You do not receive eternal life by working for it or by trying to make yourself behave. You receive eternal life by believing the record God gave of His son. Remember, if you disagree with these statements you are calling God a liar.

"...He that believes not God has made Him a liar; because he believes not the record that God gave of His Son. And this is the record, that God has given to us eternal life, and this life is in His Son." (I John 5:10,11)

God, in His Sovereignty, permits man's destiny to depend on man's choice.

"He that believes on Him is not condemned: but he that believes not is condemned already, because he has not believed in the Name of the only begotten Son of God." (John 3:18)

AFTER you are saved, obedience to God brings love, joy, peace and happiness into your life (see Galatians 5:22,23).

When we disobey God, He will punish us, but our punishment will never be hell. God deals with us as a father deals with his son. (See I Corinthians 3:15; 5:5; 11:32).

God will never cast us out or lose us.

"...Him that comes to Me I will in no wise cast out...all which He has given Me I should lose nothing, but should raise it up again at the last day." (John 6:37,39)

Doesn't it make sense to believe on the One who came back from the dead and trust Him for the payment of your sin? Why not do it now and you can be sure of going to heaven when you die. He loves you. Right now, why not accept the payment He has made for your sins and you can KNOW you have eternal life.

"These things I have written unto you that believe on the Name of the Son of God; that you may KNOW that you have eternal life..." (I John 5:13)

Christ Died...That's History

Christ Died For Me...That's Salvation!

"For God so loved the world that He gave His only begotten Son, that _____ whosoever (your name) believes in Him should not perish, but have everlasting life." (John 3:16)

Friend, if you can sincerely put your name in the blank space above, on the authority of God's Word, you can KNOW you have eternal life.

"Verily, verily (Truthfully, truthfully) I say unto you, he that believes on ME HAS (possesses now) everlasting life." (John 6:47)

If you have received Christ as your savior, please let us know.

Having something in your hand to give to someone will usually gain favorable attention. Most people willingly accept a tract.

While undoubtedly any clear salvation tract can be used in your witnessing, we have pictured in this chapter the "Heaven" tract, which has proven exceptionally effective as a conversation opener, because of its probing title, "Am I Going to Heaven?"

If you have only a few moments, you can simple give this pamphlet to someone with a remark such as, "I'd like to give this to you to read. I think you will find it very interesting."

When people receive this tract, they almost invariably ask a question or make a comment about it-and this is your direct lead into the plan of salvation. Often they will say something like, "Not me, I'll never make it to heaven." This is fine, because then you know they already realize THEIR works are unable to make them fit for heaven.

If you have the time, it is well to go over the tract with them first, explaining that while the list contains many wonderful things to do, the Bible says good works cannot save a person, and that they need to trust Christ as the One who has made complete payment for their sins. Show them John 3:16 on the back page and how they can put their name in the blank space when they believe in Christ as their Saviour.

This tract is not copyrighted. The original author has given his permission for the tract to be used by others. It has been revised twice from the original form. We know of over two million copies of this tract that have been given out. Because of its unusual clarity in presenting the plan of salvation, and because of its tremendously fruitful results, we encourage you to use it also. Your group can have these tracts printed by an offset press. If you would like a few sample copies, you may write to Pastor Wally Morillo, P.O. Box 775, Pharr, TX 78577.

We think you will be pleased with the way it will increase your ministry.

Note: May we suggest that if you are leaving a tract with a tip for a waiter or waitress, that you leave a generous tip. They will probably be more inclined to read it because of your kindness to them.

THE "GOOD NEWS" CARD-UNIQUE CONVERSATION OPENER

Everybody likes to hear good news, and this idea has been incorporated into a telephone ministry called TEL-EVANGELISM, using short recordings of the plan of salvation.

USING TEL-EVANGELISM AS A CONVERSATION OPENER

Miami, Florida, was the experimental city for a new kind of ministry, TEL-EVANGELISM, which, as the name implies, is evangelism by telephone and is an excellent conversation opener with the "good news" card to be handed out. For information on how your group can have this unique, inexpensive ministry write: TEL-EVANGELISM, Inc., Rev. Herbert Paynter, 3313 Fowler Blvd., Lawrenceville, GA 30244 (404) 921-5078.

Printed below is a sample "TEL-ADULT" message:

"Thank you for calling. This is a recording of the best news you could hear. First, ask yourself this question: 'Where are you going when you die?' Have you ever wondered if some of the things you have done would keep you from going to heaven? You can know right now whether or not you are going to heaven or hell. The reason you can know now is because your destination of heaven or hell does not depend on what you do. It depends upon your acceptance of what God has already done for you.

"The good news is that God tells us He saves us by paying for our sins and giving us eternal life. Look up and study carefully Ephesians 2:8, 9, 'For by grace are ye saved through faith; and that not of yourselves: it is the gift of God: Not of works, lest any man should boast.'

"Amazing, isn't it? But God said that He would save us through faith, not what we do ourselves. It is the gift of God. This means that it is free to us, because God has paid the price.

"Why not take God at His Word and believe that 'God so loved the world, that He gave His only begotten Son, that whosoever believeth in Him should not perish, but have everlasting life.' This would make you God's child-this believing in Him-and then, when you disobey Him you would certainly receive punishment, but He would never lose you or cast you out. God guarantees this to us in John 6:37 and 39. If you trust Christ as your Saviour, God will deal with you as His son, and while the punishment for what you do wrong will never be hell, because you are now His child, He will chasten you because He loves you.

"To have eternal life you do not have to join a church or pay money; in fact, you can do nothing to earn eternal life. You simply accept the payment for your sins that God has already made for you. Believe the record God gave of His Son.

"You can trust Him. Why not, right now, silently, tell God you believe that He paid for your sins on the cross, just like He said He did. Right now, receive Christ as your Saviour. God bless you."

You can see that the message is a non-denominational, clear, gospel presentation with an invitation to receive Christ as Saviour at the end. The person is then invited to call your church or your appointed counselor to receive further information or to have any questions he might have answered from the Bible. This "call back" number has proven very valuable because the caller then receives Scriptural counsel from a qualified soulwinner. This soulwinner could be some one confined to bed, a housewife, or anyone who wants an opportunity to witness to those actively seeking the Lord Jesus Christ.

The soulwinners using TEL-EVANGELISM report that over 90% of those who call this "call back" number indicate they are accepting Christ as their Saviour.

Using this "good news" card as a conversation opener is really unusually effective, for while some people will refuse a tract, almost everyone is pleased to receive this "good news" card. People want to hear good news! This card seems to cause an instant rapport, as well as to arouse an interest and desire in the person to hear more about this "good news."

Very often the person will ask questions that you can answer directly with the plan of salvation... and from the conversations opened many have received Christ as their Saviour even before they had the opportunity to call the TEL-EVANGELISM number!

THE CLOSE-THE INVITATION TIME

It is extremely important not to try to close before the person understands the plan of salvation. When you feel sure he understands the gospel and you are ready to ask him to trust Christ as his Saviour, then do so. Don't wait.

Here is a sample conversation:

THE WITNESS: "Does what I have been saying make sense to you?"

THE LOST: "Yes, it does."

THE WITNESS: "Since it makes sense to you, wouldn't you like to receive Christ as your Saviour right now?"

THE LOST: "Yes, I would like to do that."

THE WITNESS: "All right, the best you know how, do you really believe Jesus was the Lord and that He paid for all your sin?"

THE LOST: "Yes, I do."

THE WITNESS: "I am so glad, because when you believe this God says you can KNOW you have eternal life. Look at this verse: I John 5:13, 'These things have I written unto you that believe on the Name of the Son of God, that ye may KNOW that ye have eternal life....'"

Each of these questions that you have been asking this person should receive a "yes" response. This is because by this time he should understand the gospel, or you wouldn't be asking him to receive Christ as his Saviour yet. If at any point in your "close" the person should say "no," it doesn't make sense, or "no" he doesn't want to receive Christ as his Saviour, you should ask him why he feels that way and answer his objections with Scripture. Then when you again feel he understands, invite him to receive Christ as his Saviour.

If for some reason the lost persistently refuses to trust the Lord, or if he seems really set against pursuing the subject of salvation, it may be best to let the subject "drop" for the time being. But I would certainly caution such a person with a remark such as, "You know, you are in a very precarious position, rejecting the Lord who loves you so much. If I were you, I would certainly give this much thought and not waste any time coming to a decision, because if you were to die now, in your present condition, you would go to hell." This must be done in love, though firmly. You could use a verse like John 3:18, showing him he is condemned because of his unbelief.

An effective way to get the person to see the error of NOT accepting Christ as his Saviour is to use I John 5:10, "He that believeth on the Son of God hath the witness in himself: he that believeth not God HATH MADE HIM A LIAR: because he believeth not the record that GOD gave of His Son."

Most people will readily admit they wouldn't call God a liar. And yet, if they don't believe what the Bible says about Christ and salvation, that is exactly what they are doing.

Use I John 5:9 which says "If we receive the witness of men, the witness of God is GREATER...." Every time we go into the grocery store and buy something in a can, we "receive the witness of men" when we believe that the label on the can TELLS THE TRUTH about what is in the can. When we buy tomato soup we never stop to worry if maybe it will turn out to be onion soup. We take the company at its word. We are receiving the witness of men.

When a boy tells a girl he is going to marry her, the girl accepts his word, and they become "engaged." She believes her young man is telling the truth. She isn't calling him a liar. She receives the "witness" of this man. Sometimes people make mistakes. Sometimes they will be wrong. Sometimes they will even lie. But the Bible says if we receive the witness of men, who are fallible, HOW MUCH MORE we should receive the witness of God who is infallible-who never makes a mistake-who never lies (Titus 1:2; Psalm 18:30).

Occasionally a person is so obstinate, and even blasphemous toward the Lord that a statement like, "If you died in your present condition and didn't go to hell, it would be the first time the Bible ever made a mistake," is necessary for him to realize the gravity of the situation that he is in.

It amazes me how seemingly totally indifferent some people are to the gospel. Romans, chapter one, verses 18-32 give us a picture, a horrible picture, of unsaved mankind. You could call it "evolution in reverse." When man was created, he had fellowship with God. But mankind has gone downward, not upward. Atheism and idolatry don't come from ignorance (Rom. 1:19, 20, 28) but from WILLFUL refusal of the truth.

When you are asking a person to receive Christ as his Saviour, do not ask him to join your church. Don't confuse church membership with salvation. AFTER he is saved you might recommend a good church to him.

During the invitation to receive the Lord, don't ask him to change his life or to make any promises to God. This has nothing to do with his salvation and will only confuse the issue in his mind.

The invitation time is one of the most CRUCIAL times in your witnessing. You can either drive the person from Christ or lead him to Christ as a result of what you say, the way you say it, and how you word it.

Many people, having a sincere desire to see the person come to have the joys of serving the Lord, speak of salvation and service in the "same breath," and we have heard many, many testimonies of those who had heard this kind of invitation, who testify they were never saved under that preaching, but were only confused, made bitter, and caused to think they could never be saved because they didn't think they could change the way they were living.

Preach the gospel of salvation by grace through faith... God the Holy Spirit will save the person, indwell his life, and give him the power then to live a life pleasing to the Lord. "For it is God which worketh in you, both to will and to do of His good pleasure" (Phil. 2:13).

ONE CAUTION: You will do harm to the new Christian to TELL him he will go to heaven, without having him see it for himself in the Bible. His assurance shouldn't come from the word of any person, but from the Word of the Lord.

CHAPTER VI—Repentance

The Importance Of Repentance

What place should repentance have in your presentation of the gospel? Is repentance the same thing as belief? Or is it something distinct from it? Is it important to emphasize repentance, or should we never mention it in this age of grace? What does repentance really mean, anyway? These are some of the questions the soulwinner must face (and answer) regarding the subject of repentance.

There can be little doubt that all men, from Adam on, have had to repent in order to have a right relationship with God. The importance of this is brought home when we realize men of every Biblical age preached it. John the Baptist preached it (Mark 1:15); the Apostle John proclaimed its necessity (Rev. 2:5); Paul preached repentance wherever he went (Acts 17:30; 20:21); and the Lord Jesus Christ Himself strongly emphasized that men who refused to repent would perish (Luke 13:3, 5). So, you see, repentance is necessary for salvation.

The Misuse Of The Word

The question is, "What does the Bible MEAN by 'repent,' and how should it be presented to the lost?" The important thing is NOT what repentance has COME to mean down through the centuries since Christ's time, but rather-and this is of utmost importance-what the word did mean WHEN IT WAS SPOKEN by Christ, Paul, Peter, and others in Biblical times.

If you look up "repent" or "repentance" in a modern dictionary you will read definitions like the following: "regret; to feel sorry for sin and seek forgiveness; to turn from sin." Based on these definitions, preachers have been going about earnestly trying to get men to quit their sinning, or at least to work up a genuine sorrow for sin. But is this the divinely appointed task of Christians to get men to change their ways?

No! This kind of preaching often leads to a form of self-righteousness and self-reformation-not to salvation. Does a sinner have to turn from or give up his sins to be saved? COULD he do this? Did you? Have you yet given up all sinning? "If we say that we have no sin, we deceive ourselves, and the truth is not in us" (I John 1:8).

It is sadly apparent that our modern-day misuse of the word "repent" has done a great deal of harm and has confused multitudes. Because of the wrong use of the word "repent" men have gotten the idea that a Christian is one who doesn't smoke, drink, curse, go to dances or movies, or do anything that is wrong or immoral.

This negativism has blinded people to the fact that a Christian is "one of Christ's"-one who, through faith, has received Christ as his Saviour. Once a person has Christ and His power in his life, THEN his behavior often changes. But this change is the RESULT of being a child of God; it is not the CAUSE.

Being good is not the way to become a child of God. Remember Ephesians 2: 8, 9, "For by grace are ye saved through faith; and that not of yourselves: it is the gift of God: Not of works, lest any man should boast."

Because preachers have allowed themselves to propagate this error in the teaching of repentance, our churches are full of "good," self-righteous, moral people who are certain they are "Christians," yet when they are asked if they are going to heaven, the best answer they can give is, "I hope so."

They do not have the assurance that comes from knowing Christ as their Saviour. Instead, they are plagued by the uncertainty that comes from trying to be good enough by their own efforts to gain heaven.

All too often this idea that "I must be good to gain God's favor" comes from Bible-believing men who preach that one must either "turn from sin or burn in hell." How sad and tragic it is that so much damage can be caused by the misuse of one word.

The Correct Meaning of "Repent"

The word in the New Testament usually translated "repent" is the Greek word "metanoeo," and the word translated "repentance" is "metanoia." Both of these Greek words have the same basic meaning: "to change your mind; reconsider; or, to think differently."

Granted, if a person changes his mind (repents) toward certain sins in his life, he may become very sorrowful and may even stop those particular outward sins, but the sorrow and the ceasing from certain sins would be the RESULT of repenting, not repentance itself.

When God tells an unsaved man to repent, He means for that man to change his mind about how to reach God and accept GOD'S way of salvation. The person must CHANGE HIS MIND from any idea of religion he may have to save him, and trust Christ's payment for everything he has done wrong.

Passages on Repentance Explained

Luke 13:1-5, "There were present at that season some that told Him of the Galileans, whose blood Pilate had mingled with their sacrifices. And Jesus answering said unto them, Suppose ye that these Galileans were sinners above all the Galileans, because they suffered such things? I tell you, Nay: but except ye repent (change your mind) ye shall all likewise perish (i.e., like these Galileans did). Or those eighteen, upon whom the tower in Siloam fell, and slew them, think ye that they were sinners above all men that dwelt in Jerusalem? I tell you, Nay: but, except ye repent (change your mind), ye shall all likewise perish."

Try to get the picture. Christ in this passage was talking to good people who believed the old tradition that people suffered only because of their sins. So they logically concluded that those in Galilee and at the Tower of Siloam who died such horrible deaths must have been great sinners.

Christ contradicts what they "suppose" (v. 2) and "think" (v. 4) and tells these self-righteous people that they need to change their minds and see themselves as sinners, too. Christ is not saying "Turn from your sin," but that they should recognize that they are sinners, or they will perish in their own self-righteousness.

Even if one doesn't know Greek, it is obvious from the passage itself that the meaning of "repent" here cannot be "sorrow for," or "turning from, sin." These people obviously needed, above all else, to think differently-in this case, to think differently about themselves, about others, and about God.

Acts 17:30, "And the times of this ignorance God winked at (or, overlooked); but now commandeth all men everywhere to repent."

To understand what God means here by "repent" only requires one to read the last part of verse 29 of the same chapter, "we ought not TO THINK that the Godhead is like unto... silver, or stone, graven by art and man's device." Instead, what ought these philosophers of Mars' Hill to think? They needed to CHANGE THEIR MINDS and see that God is quite different from stone!. He is judge (v. 31), and He is alive (vv. 31, 32). Again, from the context, the true meaning of "repent" is clear.

Acts 20:20, 21, "And how I kept back nothing that was profitable unto you, but have shewed you, and have taught you publicly, and from house to house, Testifying both to the Jews and also to the Greeks, repentance toward God, and faith toward our Lord Jesus Christ."

Notice that the Bible states here that we are to proclaim repentance TOWARD GOD. There is nothing here about turning from sin. Paul is giving his last words to these be loved Ephesian elders whom he had led to Christ. They had formerly been heathen idol worshipers (Acts 19) and very immoral. However, Paul's preaching to them was that they needed to change their thinking about God.

Think what an impact on these sinful heathen the truth of Romans 5:8 would have had: "But God commendeth (displayed) His love toward us, in that, WHILE WE WERE YET SINNERS, Christ died for us."

Remember, the word "gospel" means "good news." Do you think it would have been good news to them if Paul had said, "While we were trying to give up our sins, God tried to love us a little bit," or, "While we were yet sinners, Christ died for our past sins, and now if we stop all our present sins and never commit any sins in the future, God will love us"?

No! These sinners needed to know that the God of the universe loved them even as they were. They needed the assurance that God was not requiring of them the impossible -that they stop sinning-but simply that they would trust Christ and His payment for their sins and thus receive salvation.

Later Scripture makes it clear that God certainly did work in their lives to bring about changes, but this took place only AFTER they were already saved (Eph. 2:10).

Acts 2:38, "Then Peter said unto them, Repent, and be baptized every one of you in the Name of Jesus Christ for the remission of sins, and ye shall receive the GIFT of the Holy Ghost."

Chapter Nine covers the part of this verse dealing with baptism. Here we will concentrate on the part of the verse having to do with repentance. One of the first rules to follow in understanding any Bible verse is to consider the context. In the second chapter of Acts we discover that these Jewish unbelievers thought the disciples were drunk (vv. 13, 15) and that Jesus was only a man whom they crucified (vv. 23, 36). Peter lets them know that the disciples were not drunk but in God's will (vv. 15-17), that Jesus is the Christ (Messiah) sent by God, and that even though men crucified Him, God raised Him from the dead (vv. 24, 32, 36).

These Jewish men, having been set straight on these matters, were "pricked in their heart (Greek, 'thoughts') and said unto Peter and to the rest of the apostles, Men and brethren, what shall we do?" (v. 37)

Peter's immediate answer was, "Repent... every one of you... for the remission of sins...." In the frenzy of the day that Jesus stood before Pilate the mob had cried, "Crucify Him, crucify Him." Then they saw Him only as a man and a troublemaker. Now Peter tells them they must repent (think differently) toward this One and realize that He is "both Lord and Christ" (v. 36), and that salvation comes only through Him (vv. 21, 38, 41). This, again, is Biblical repentance.

USING "REPENTANCE" IN WITNESSING

If you are going to use the word "repent" or "repentance" in your witnessing, you should always explain what it really means. You can perhaps teach the meaning of repentance through your personal testimony, explaining that you used to think God hated sin so much that He hated you as well, and not until you heard the gospel did you understand that God loves you and wants you to go to heaven. (If this IS part of your testimony.) Then, after understanding the gospel, you began to think differently about God. This way you could have the person understand the plan of salvation... he could repent... and you would never have to worry about whether or not you confused him by the word "repent."

The important thing in witnessing is to lead the lost person from wherever he is spiritually to having faith in Christ as his Saviour. You should try to do this as smoothly and naturally as possible. Using first or third person illustrations in your conversation is an excellent way of achieving the desired results, and particularly in giving a proper, Scriptural explanation of repentance.

That great giant of the faith Dr. William L. Pettingill put it well in his book, Bible Questions Answered. Under Repentance and Salvation, page 215, he answers the following question: "What place has repentance in salvation? Should we tell people to repent of their sins to be saved?"

"The Gospel of John is the Holy Spirit's Gospel tract, written that men might believe that Jesus is the Christ, the Son of God; and that believing they might have life through His Name (20: 31). And it does not mention the word 'repentance.' But that is only because repentance is a necessary part of saving faith. Strictly speaking, the word repentance means a 'change of mind.' It is by no means the same thing as sorrow (II Cor. 7:10). Since it is not possible for an unbeliever to become a believer without changing his mind, it is therefore unnecessary to say anything about it. The only thing for a man to do in order to be saved is to believe on the Lord Jesus Christ: and to believe on Him is the same thing as receiving Him (John 1:11-13)."

Any teaching that demands a change of conduct toward either God or man for salvation is to add works or human effort to faith, and this contradicts all Scripture and is an accursed message (Gal. 1:8, 9; Deut. 27:18). Study the book of Galatians.

Remember, the closer a counterfeit comes to the truth, the more people it will fool. Don't be fooled. Yes, a Christian should make every effort to discipline his life, to lay aside every weight and the sins which so easily beset him, but this has to do with SERVICE, which can come only AFTER salvation. Salvation is always a gift; it is nothing we do ourselves.

Let's make salvation as clear as we possibly can. If something might possibly confuse someone, let's find some other way of expressing the truth so that it will be crystal clear instead of confusing.

"Beware lest any man spoil you through philosophy and vain deceit, after the tradition of men, after the rudiments of the world, and not after Christ" (Col. 2:8).

"But I fear, lest by any means, as the serpent beguiled Eve through his subtilty, so your minds should be corrupted from the SIMPLICITY that is in Christ" (II Cor. 11:3).

CHAPTER VII—"LORDSHIP SALVATION"

CHRIST, THE SAVIOUR

Jesus Christ is the only Saviour of mankind there is. "There is none other Name under heaven given among men, whereby we must be saved" (Acts 4:12). When He was born, the angel declared, "Unto you is born this day in the city of David a Saviour which is Christ the Lord" (Luke 2: 11). The prophet Isaiah quotes God as saying, "I, even I, am the LORD; and beside Me there is no Saviour" (Isaiah 43: 11).

The Scriptures are emphatic that God took on flesh in the person of the Son, Jesus Christ, and became man's Saviour (John 1:1-3, 14, 29).

Man's belief or lack of belief in the Saviourship of Jesus does not change the fact that Jesus Christ is truly the Saviour. However, when a man recognizes that Jesus Christ is truly the Saviour and trusts Him to be his Saviour, then-and only then-does that man receive the benefits of Christ's saving power.

Christ died and rose again for all (Hebrews 2:9; I John 2:2), but He saves only those who trust Him. That is to say, even though He is the "Saviour of the world," He saves only those in the world who personally and individually receive Him by faith. God invites "whosoever will" to trust in His Son, but it is an amazing truth of God's Word that men can forbid the Saviour to save them. Such men die without a Saviour, though One was available to them all the time (John 3:16-18; I John 5:10-12; Revelation 22:17).

Christ, the Lord

What we have seen about Christ being the Saviour also applies to His Lordship. He IS the Lord, whether men believe it or not. Whether or not a man allows Christ to be his Lord is something else again.

Jesus Christ is the all-knowing, all-powerful Creator and Controller of the universe. Colossians 1:16 says, "All things were created by Him and for Him." Verse 17 adds, "... by Him all things consist... (or, are held together)." God led Paul to write that Jesus Christ is the "blessed and only Potentate, the King of kings, and Lord of lords" (I Tim. 6:15). The One who was crucified on Calvary was none other than the Lord of Glory (I Cor. 2:8).

Some may ask if Jesus was really LORD when men "by wicked hands crucified" Him. Absolutely! For He said, "... I lay down My life, that I might take it again. No man taketh it from Me, but I lay it down of Myself, I have power to lay it down, and I have power to take it again..." (John 10:17, 18).

Is He Lord now, though some men refuse to let Him rule in their lives? Certainly! The Bible says, "... know assuredly that God hath made that same Jesus, whom ye have crucified, both Lord and Christ (Messiah)." The time is coming when EVERYONE will confess that Jesus Christ is Lord (Phil. 2:10, 11).

The Issue Involved

Just as you receive the Saviour by faith and He becomes YOUR Saviour, when you allow Christ to control your life, He becomes YOUR LORD. There is an increasing number of "evangelicals" today who are preaching that in order for a man to be saved he must not only receive Christ as his Saviour, but also must make Him absolute Lord and Master of his life.

This doctrine has been termed "Lordship salvation" and has absolutely no support from the Word of God. It is, in fact, another subtle way Satan has invented to get Bible-believing men to add works to salvation without, perhaps, their realizing it, and to do it in such a way that it sounds spiritual and good.

What could SOUND more spiritual or honoring to the Lord than statements like: "Either Christ is Lord of all, or He is not Lord at all. And if He is not Lord then He is not your Saviour. You are lost. You must turn over all the strings of your life to Him—then He will save you. Give your life to Him if you want to be truly saved." This is what is taught.

The truth of the matter is that salvation is not a "give" proposition at all; it is a "take" proposition. We don't give our hearts, lives, wills, or anything else to God in order to get Him to save us. This would be a form of bribery, a way of meriting or deserving to be saved—but God says salvation is "NOT OF OURSELVES"-and especially, it is not offering anything to God.

Salvation is receiving! We simply receive His Son. John 1:12 says, "But as many as RECEIVED Him, to them gave He power (the right) to become the sons of God, even to them that believe on His Name." God does the giving. We do the receiving.

God GAVE His Son (John 3:16).

God GIVES eternal life to those who trust His Son (John 10:28).

God GIVES believers everything they need through His Son (Rom. 8:32).

Christ didn't come to have us sacrifice, or minister, or give our life to Him... but He came to be OUR sacrifice, to minister to US, and to give His life a ransom payment for OUR sin. "For even the Son of man came not to be ministered unto, but to minister, and to give His life a ransom for many" (Mark 10:45).

God offers to save us as sinners and doesn't require us to stop sinning and start obeying Him before He saves us. "But God commendeth His love toward us, in that, while we were yet sinners, Christ died for us." I John 1:8 tells us that "If we say that we have no sin, we deceive ourselves, and the truth is not in us." No one can say that he stopped his sinning and THEN the Lord saved him. It is impossible. Be careful not to ask a person to do the impossible. Remember, God did not require it of you either. It is only after a person is saved that the Holy Spirit will give him the power to control his old nature and live a life pleasing to the Lord (Phil. 2:13).

"Lordship salvation" is sometimes preached by men who are sincerely sick of the low spiritual level of the "average" Christian. So these men begin preaching a message they hope will bring more lasting and noticeable results. We can sympathize with these preachers. The spiritual condition of believers is often deplorable. But even a casual reading of the New Testament reveals that the early church had the same problems. See I Cor. 3:1-4; 5:1-5; Gal. 4:8-11; Heb. 5:12 14; and II Thess. 3:6-15.

What did the early apostles do to combat this problem of spiritual weakness? Did they change the gospel message from "Believe on the Lord Jesus Christ and thou shalt be saved" to "Believe on the Lord Jesus Christ, give up sin, and let Him rule over all the details of your life, and thou shalt be saved"? Of course not! That isn't the gospel! God doesn't give the Holy Spirit in response to a "grace plus works" message for salvation.

What did the apostles do? They emphasized the proper doctrines to meet the needs of the people. Such great life transforming truths as the Holy Spirit of God indwelling the believer, Christ's at-any-moment return, the eternal destiny of the lost, and the fact that "every one of us must give account of himself to God"-these were brought to bear on the children of God, and the Holy Spirit did His work of convicting and changing lives.

The problem does not lie with God's message of salvation. That is eternal and unchanging. It will always be sufficient to do what it is intended to do-to save souls. The problem is that God's people have not had the great Biblical truths applied to their lives, and so they are living at a spiritually low ebb.

If a person has to make Christ Lord of his life to be saved, why are most of the New Testament epistles filled with commands, warnings, exhortations, and pleas for the child of God to yield to Christ's Lordship? If "Lordship salvation" were true, these people wouldn't even be children of God! But it is apparent that they are, for throughout the epistles they are called "brethren," "saints," "believers," etc.

Now since it is obvious that God DOES exhort His own children to ALLOW Him to control them, to be their Lord, then it is just as obvious that they did not HAVE to make Him Lord in order to be saved. Consider these passages where God pleads with His own children to allow Him to control them: Rom. 6:12, 13; 12:1, 2; Gal. 5:16; 3:1-3; Eph. 4:1-3; 6:10-17. When the pastor FEEDS his sheep they will not lack knowing how to be spiritual (Jer. 23:4, 28; Acts 20:18-32; II Tim. 4:2).

Consideration of Romans 10:9

This is the primary verse used to try to prove the teaching of "Lordship salvation." The King James translation reads, "That if thou shalt confess with thy mouth the Lord Jesus, and shalt believe in thine heart that God hath raised Him from the dead, thou shalt be saved." A more literal rendering of part of this verse is, "That if thou shalt confess with thy mouth Jesus as Lord... thou shalt be saved." This is where the advocates of "Lordship salvation" get their basis for the doctrine.

However, notice several things about the context of this verse. First of all, Paul is writing primarily of unbelieving Israel. From a human standpoint, the Jews had a very real part in crucifying Christ; see Acts 2:22, 23, 36; 4:10-12. Had they realized that Jesus was God Himself, they certainly would not have had a part in His death (I Cor. 2:7, 8). Therefore, unbelieving Jews (and anyone else who wants to be saved) must own up to the fact that Jesus is the Lord- that He is God Himself-and all who call upon Him this way are saved (Romans 10:9, 10, 13). The emphasis here is not upon making Jesus Lord of someone's life, but rather on recognizing His true identity-that He is God! In John 8:24 we find that if a person doesn't believe Christ is God, he will die in his sins.

Notice, too, that nowhere in the entire chapter of Romans 10 are our lives in view. Instead, the emphasis is on His person. The issue here is not so much what I do, but who He is. The question is not one of service but of salvation. Never confuse the two. Salvation becomes ours when we trust Christ to SAVE us. Effective service is ours through OBEDIENCE. Salvation primarily involves the spirit and our eternal destiny; it is a gift (John 5: 24). Service involves the body and our present earthly life; it is labor for which rewards are given (Rom. 12:1, 2; I Cor. 3:8-15; Luke 10:2).

The late Dr. M. R. DeHaan realized the importance of keeping salvation and service separate and said so well: "There is a vast difference between coming to Jesus for salvation and coming after Jesus for service. Coming to Christ makes one a believer, while coming after Christ makes one a disciple. All believers are not disciples. To become a believer one accepts the invitation of the Gospel. To be a disciple one obeys the challenge of a life of dedicated service and separation.

Salvation comes through the sacrifice of Christ, but discipleship comes only by sacrifice of self and surrender to His call for devoted service. Salvation is free, but discipleship involves paying the price of a separated walk. Salvation cannot be lost, because it depends upon God's faithfulness, but discipleship can be lost, because it depends upon our faithfulness."

Reasons for Not Teaching "Lordship Salvation"

1. It contradicts Scripture; therefore, it cannot be true. This one reason should settle the matter completely. If a doctrine is contrary to what God says, then it should be discarded immediately. See Rom. 3:4; Titus 2:7; Gal. 4:16.

2. It causes confusion and frustration to the unbeliever because it leaves the impression that salvation is by works. Therefore, the lost person often puts off accepting Christ until he is "ready" to turn his entire life over to the Lord. If the truth were presented to such a person, that salvation is free, but that after we are saved the Lord would work in our lives, perhaps he would trust Christ. Because of a "grace plus works" message he might NEVER trust Christ (I Cor. 14:8,9).

3. This message CANNOT SAVE. If anyone gets saved during such a message, it will be because God has honored a portion of His Word IN SPITE of the unscriptural teaching brought into the message (Rom. 4:5; Gal. 5:1-4; Rom. 11:6; Isa. 55:8-11; Rom.10:17).

4. This message is accursed of God. Any message, no matter how "good" it may sound, is condemned by God unless it is His own salvation message. HIS message is the only one that saves. All others are of satanic or fleshly origin and curse men to hell. Therefore, God curses such a message (Acts 4:12; John 14:6; Gal. 1:6-9; II Cor. 11:13 15; Gal. 3:1-3).

5. The person who preaches such a message is also accursed of God. Strong statement? Yes, but it is what God says. A man who preaches man's efforts have a part in salvation is leading people to hell, not heaven. Even if a man believes he is sincere, a wrong message still has the effects of the wrong message. Sincerity is no substitute for truth (Deut. 27:18; Prov. 17:15; 19:5; Jer. 23:1).

6. It, in effect, makes God a liar and the Bible untrue. If salvation really does come to those who turn over their lives to Christ, then God has been wrong all the time, throughout the entire Bible, because salvation is taught from Genesis to Revelation to come only through faith (Titus 1:2, 3; Romans 3: 4).

7. It causes even Christian preachers to further the error by thinking it might have some merit and preaching it themselves. One well-known Christian returned to America from some meetings he held in a foreign country and made a statement like this: "I really made it difficult for them to accept Christ over there. In America it's too easy to become a Christian, so I made it hard for them there. I told them accepting Christ meant turning from their sins, reading their Bibles, praying every day, giving up bad habits, and going to church regularly. And in spite of such a hard message hundreds made decisions for Christ."

WHAT A TRAGEDY! When people hear the true gospel after hearing this type of message, they are often unable to distinguish what is truth from what is error, and so many are left confused and unsaved.

8. The preaching of this error robs the one preaching it of reward. Paul said, "What is our... crown? Are not even ye in the presence of our Lord Jesus Christ at His coming?" The more we are able to win to Christ, the more souls will be in heaven, and so the more reward we will have. But those who preach a confused message hinder people from trusting Christ as their Saviour. Therefore, many souls are left unsaved, and so these preachers will not have the reward that they could have had (I Thess. 2: 19, 20; II John 8; I John 2:28; I Cor. 9:18).

9. It confuses "laymen" believers and causes them to be ineffective in their witness. A girl recently asked, "I know that you are sincere and seem to have Scripture to back up what you teach, but my pastor is also sincere and teaches differently about salvation than you do. How do I know which one of you is right? How can I witness when I don't know what to tell people?"

A confused believer isn't going to be a faithful witness because he is going to be in constant turmoil over what to say. When he does try to witness, he will probably give out some mixture of "grace and works" that will not only confuse the lost person, but will also bring discouragement to the believer when he doesn't find people responding to his witness. When the gospel is given out, pure and simple, there will be results. The gospel is good news, and people respond to it.

10. It hinders the growth of the body of Christ. This is one of the results of the above (#9). When the believer's mouth is stopped (regardless of the reason), then the natural flow of fruit-bearing is stopped. Since Christ's body is composed of believers, the growth of His body is hindered when souls are not won (John 15: 8, 16).

Incidentally, this will also stop the growth of the local church as well. It is so obvious when you stop to think about it. Why any preacher thinks this accursed "grace and works" message would in any way benefit anyone is a puzzle to me. Let's learn to THINK THINGS THROUGH!

11. It brings persecution to the believers who stand firm for the Scriptural message of "justification by faith." Those who are clear on the gospel are often accused of preaching "easy believism" or "cheap grace." Nothing could be further from the truth! Tell me, is a person ever saved by "hard" believism? Certainly no Christian I know believes in "cheap" grace! This is absurd. God's grace is precious. The blood of Jesus is precious. The price our Lord paid for our redemption was so high that nothing can be compared with its great value. Salvation is anything but cheap. It is free to us only because Jesus paid the full price. And that price was His precious life blood (I Peter 1:18, 19).

God has gone through so MUCH to provide redemption for us! When I think that Jesus even gave His life-died such a horrible death-in order to provide eternal life as a free gift to those who would accept His payment by faith... and then someone comes along who professes to be a child of God and wants to make salvation HARD for the lost person... how the heart of our dear Saviour must break!

"Of how much sorer punishment, suppose ye, shall he be thought worthy, who hath trodden under foot the Son of God, and hath counted the blood of the covenant, where with he was sanctified, an unholy thing, and hath done despite unto the Spirit of grace?" (Heb. 10: 29)

I doubt seriously if anyone could carefully read the Gospel accounts of what Christ went through to purchase our salvation and ever again speak glibly of "cheap grace." No one is ever saved by "cheap grace." They are saved by PRICELESS, AMAZING GRACE! Don't let Satan blind you to the fact that salvation REALLY IS FREE to man. Don't listen to him when he insinuates that "justification by faith" is a dangerous doctrine that will lead to "loose living." The greatest soulwinners who ever lived believed in salvation by grace through faith, and they preached it faithfully... and God blessed them and their ministry for it.

We have a miracle salvation-provided and preserved by God Himself! Let's give out the good news of this salvation simply and faithfully for His glory.

"But of Him are ye in Christ Jesus, who of God is made unto us wisdom, and righteousness, and sanctification, and redemption: That, according as it is written, He that glorieth, let him glory in the Lord" (I Cor. 1:30, 31).

CHAPTER VIII—FAITH WITHOUT WORKS

James 2:14-24 is a passage frequently questioned by the lost after they hear the gospel of salvation through faith without works.

Actually, to receive proper understanding of this passage is not difficult when one keeps in mind some simple principles valuable in discerning any Scripture:

1. To whom is the author writing... lost or saved people?

2. What situation prompted the writing of this passage?

3. A careful study of the passage, verse by verse, not adding to or taking away from the Word of God.

4. Comparison of this passage with other passages in the Bible on the same particular issue.

Looking at James 2:14-24 from the above standpoints we find:

1. It is written to the saved, to believers. In verse 14 James says "my brethren."

2. This entire epistle is written to Christians for their instruction on conduct and Christian service.

3. Below is a verse-by-verse consideration of the passage. James 2:14, "What doth it profit, my brethren, though a man say he hath faith, and have not works? Can faith save him?" James asks if there is any profit, any value, any fruit, if a man claims to have faith in Christ and yet doesn't live and serve as a Christian should.

Christians are told in Ephesians 2:10, "For we are His workmanship, created in Christ Jesus UNTO good works, which God hath before ordained that we SHOULD walk in them." It is true that those who are saved are saved by faith and not by what they do; but, AFTER they are saved, God wants them to do good works.

Titus 3: 8 points this out so clearly: "This is a faithful saying, and these things I will that thou affirm constantly, that they which have believed in God might be careful to MAINTAIN GOOD WORKS. These things are good and profitable unto men."

In order to help people and have a ministry with them a Christian must be careful to live a good testimony. Titus 3: 14 tells us, "And let ours also learn to maintain good works for necessary uses, that they be not UNFRUITFUL." If you want to bear fruit for the Lord you must do good works... not to be saved... but to be fruitful.

So to answer James's first question-There is no profit, no fruit, if a man says he has faith but doesn't produce any works. He is saved, but he is an unfruitful Christian. John 15: 2 warns those who are saved-in Christ-but do not bear fruit, "Every branch in Me that beareth not fruit He taketh away...." God removes the Christian who is a stumbling block to others.

The next question in James 2:14 is "Can faith save him?" Romans 4:5 answers this clearly: "But to him that worketh NOT, but believeth on Him that justifieth the ungodly, his faith IS COUNTED FOR RIGHTEOUSNESS." Yes, faith can save him. In fact, nothing else could. When a person tries to be saved by faith and works, he cannot be saved (Romans 11:6; Gal. 5:2; Gal. 5:4).

James 2:15, 16, "If a brother or sister be naked, and destitute of daily food, and one of you say unto them, Depart in peace, be ye warmed and filled; notwithstanding ye give them not those things which are needful to the body; what doth it profit?" The answer is that it doesn't profit that hungry person at all. You have not helped a person's material needs-you have not provided him with food or clothes-just by telling him to leave in peace.

James 2:17, "Even so faith, if it hath not works, is dead, being alone." Yes, it is true, that if you have faith in Christ, but do not work and serve the Lord, your faith will not bear FRUIT. The word "dead" in this verse is "nekros" (Greek) and means "useless." (See Greek-English Lexicon, by Arndt and Gingrich, Univ. of Chicago Press, page 536.)

If you have faith in the Lord, but you don't do anything for others, your faith will not be of any value to them. It will be useless to them. You are not demonstrating your faith in Christ to others by just telling them to "Depart in peace, be ye warmed and filled," if you are not willing to do something to help them. In fact, you will be a discredit to Christianity and do much harm to the gospel.

James 2:18, "Yea, a man may say, Thou hast faith, and I have works: shew me thy faith without thy works, and I will shew thee my faith by my works." A Christian could say, "You have faith and I have good works. You tell me you have so much faith without showing me any good works, but I will tell you I have faith, and you can SEE that I have faith because my works SHOW that I believe."

James 2:19, "Thou believest that there is one God; thou doest well: the devils also believe, and tremble." Even the devils cannot deny there is a God. But believing in God isn't enough to save. You must believe what God, the Lord Jesus Christ, has done for you and accept His payment for your sin to be saved.

James 2:20, "But wilt thou know, O vain man, that faith without works is dead?" As in v. 17, faith without works is of no use to other people. A saved person who doesn't serve the Lord lives a vain, useless Christian life. He will be chastised in this life and have no reward in the thousand year reign of Christ (Hebrews 12:6; I Cor. 3:15). He will not have love, joy, or peace in his life, as these things are not the results of living for yourself, but the results of living for the Lord, disciplining your life under the direction of, and by the power of the Holy Spirit (Galatians 5:22).

James 2: 21, "Was not Abraham our father justified by works, when he had offered Isaac his son upon the altar?" The answer to James's question here is "YES!" Yes, Abraham was justified by works WHEN he offered up Isaac. But the question is, justified BEFORE WHOM? Before men, or before God? AT THAT TIME when men saw the

great faith Abraham had, that he even offered his son to God at His request, Abraham was justified in the sight of MEN. They knew, by his works, that here was a man who truly had great faith in God. His faith was DEMONSTRATED in the sight of man by his works.

But WHEN was Abraham justified in the sight of GOD? The Lord justified Abraham by his faith MANY YEARS before he offered up Isaac. In fact, Abraham was justified before Isaac was even born! "And he believed in the Lord; and He counted it to him for righteousness" (Gen. 15:6).

Galatians 3:6-11 is very clear on this. "Even as Abraham BELIEVED God, and it was accounted to him for righteousness. Know ye therefore that they which are of FAITH, the same are the children of Abraham. And the Scripture, foreseeing that God would justify the heathen through FAITH, preached before the GOSPEL unto Abraham, saying, In thee shall all nations be blessed. So then they which be of faith are blessed with faithful Abraham. For as many as are of the works of the law are under the curse: for it is written, Cursed is every one that continueth not in all things which are written in the book of the law to do them. But that NO man is justified by the law in the sight of God, it is evident: for the just shall live by FAITH."

James 2: 22, "Seest thou how faith wrought with his works, and by works was faith made perfect?" How true and clear this verse really is. PEOPLE see, YOU see, that Abraham-through faith-through absolute trust and confidence in God-offered up his son... and this act (work) proved to people that he certainly had GREAT FAITH.

James 2:23, "And the Scripture was fulfilled which saith, Abraham believed God, and it was imputed unto him for righteousness: and he was called the Friend of God." The Scripture that was fulfilled is Genesis 15:6, "And he BELIEVED in the Lord, and He (God) counted it (Abraham's faith) to him for righteousness." Yes, Abraham's BELIEF was imputed to him for righteousness. God puts His righteousness to the account of the believer because He has already paid the penalty of the believer's sins.

James 2:24, "Ye see then how that by works a man is justified, and not by faith only." PEOPLE, then, see by a person's works that he has faith. PEOPLE do not have the ability that God has to see a person's faith-to know a person's mind.

I Samuel 16:7 makes this very clear, "But the Lord said unto Samuel, Look not on his countenance, or on the height of his stature; because I have refused him: for the LORD seeth not as MAN seeth: for man looketh on the outward appearance, but the Lord looketh on the heart."

To briefly summarize James 2: 14-24-This passage teaches us that if people are to REALIZE that a person has faith in the Lord Jesus Christ, they must be able to see the person's good works. Man looks at your LIFE and judges (rightly or wrongly) whether or not you have faith. Therefore, believers should take utmost care, as Titus 3:8 points out, to maintain a good testimony. This has nothing to do with the person's salvation, but it does have a lot to do with how much influence his life is going to have upon others for the Lord Jesus Christ.

4. Compare James 2: 14-24 with verses in Romans, chapter four. This chapter is speaking of the SAME person, Abraham, and the SAME issue, his justification. Was he justified by his faith or by his works?

Romans 4:1, 2, "What shall we say then that Abraham our father, as pertaining to the flesh, hath found? For if Abraham were justified by works, he hath whereof to glory; but not before God."

We just read, in James 2:21, that Abraham WAS justified by his works! Yes, indeed... WHEN he offered Isaac, his son, upon the altar, PEOPLE realized he had faith, and he was considered a great man in the sight of the people. His works justified him in the eyes of the people at that time. He could "glory" in the public acclaim of his great faith. But IN THE SIGHT OF GOD, he received justification many years before... as was pointed out... even before Isaac was born!

Although God wants us to live the right kind of lives, doing good works, serving Him, He doesn't need our good works to SHOW Him we have faith. He is a "mind reader." He knows how we really feel deep inside. Man doesn't have this ability to know perfectly the thoughts of others.

God says in Ezekiel 11:5, "... I know the things that come into your mind, every one of them." And in I Samuel 16:7, "... for the Lord seeth NOT AS MAN SEETH; for man looketh on the outward appearance, but the Lord looketh on the heart."

The question raised in Romans 4:3 is: What does the BIBLE say about Abraham's justification? "For what saith the Scripture? Abraham BELIEVED God, and it (his belief) was counted unto him for righteousness." This is referring back to Genesis 15:6, as we quoted before.

Romans 4:4, "Now to him that worketh is the reward not reckoned of grace, but of debt." Salvation is by grace. If you work for something, your pay isn't by grace; it is owed to you. A laborer gets his pay at the end of the week because he EARNED it by his work, not because of the GRACE of the employer.

But our salvation is by the GRACE of our Lord Jesus Christ, and not as the outcome of our works. And it is a good thing salvation is by grace and not of works because nobody could be perfect enough for heaven by works, anyway. If a person thinks he could get to heaven by his good works, a good question to ask him is, "How many good works do you think you have to do to go to heaven?" or "How good do you think you would have to be to go to heaven?" God says if we sin in just one thing (James 2:10) we are still imperfect, even as if we had sinned a lot.

God doesn't save anyone who is trusting Christ AND ALSO trusting his GOOD WORKS to save him. Because salvation is by grace, it cannot be of works at all. Romans 11:6, "And if by grace, then is it no more of works: otherwise grace is no more grace. But if it be of works, then is it no more grace: otherwise work is no more work." (It's like saying: "If you have ice, then you do not have steam, because if you had steam you would no longer have ice. But if you have steam, then you do not have ice, otherwise steam is no longer steam.")

In salvation, grace and works are "mutually exclusive." Satan is always trying to reverse things in people's minds. He tries to get them to think they have to work to be saved, and then tries to keep them from working after they are saved. I PRAY that you wouldn't let Satan ever confuse your message of God's saving grace!

Romans 4:5 is one of the clearest verses proving salvation is by faith, without works. Let's examine this verse phrase by phrase.

"But to him that worketh not"... To him who doesn't do ANY work at all.

"But believeth on Him that justifieth the ungodly"... But believes on Jesus who gives His righteousness to sinners.

"His faith is counted for righteousness"... God sees his faith, and because of his faith gives him righteousness.

Romans 3:28 gives God's judgment and wisdom on the matter in finality, "Therefore we CONCLUDE that a man is justified by faith WITHOUT the deeds of the law."

Then, referring back to the thirty-second Psalm, Romans 4:6-8 tells us, "Even as David also describeth the blessedness of the man, unto whom God imputeth RIGHTEOUSNESS WITHOUT WORKS, saying, Blessed are they whose iniquities are forgiven, and whose sins are covered. Blessed is the man to whom the Lord will not impute sin." Blessed is the man of whom God says, "I will not charge your sins to you. I have paid for them Myself." God says this, however, only to the man who trusts Christ alone for his salvation. God never says this to the man who tries to get to heaven by his own works, in full or in part.

In trying to lead a person to the Lord, answer his questions as briefly and simply as you can. Agree with him- Abraham WAS justified by his works-- but NOT BEFORE GOD. Go into detail only as you have to.

If the person does not, for some reason, seem to understand the true meaning of James, chapter two, even after you have explained it to him using Romans, chapter four, we recommend that you take him back to Ephesians 2:8, 9 and stay there a while. If by this time he doesn't see the light, perhaps his problem doesn't come from a particular passage like in James, but rather from a complete lack of comprehension of the plan of salvation itself. Go over it again with him. Stay with clear, positive Scriptures on salvation be cause it will still be the GOSPEL that will be the power God uses to bring him to Christ for salvation.

CHAPTER IX—WATER BAPTISM

The Roman Catholic Church, the Church of Christ, even some Lutheran churches, and a few Baptist churches teach that a person must be water baptized (as well as have faith in Christ) or he cannot be saved. As a soulwinner, you should know what the Bible says on the matter and how to answer this "objection" to trusting Christ alone for salvation.

In order to understand the Scriptural teaching regarding baptism, you must know what the word means. The Greek words translated "baptize" and "baptism" are "baptizo," "baptisma," and "baptismos." Even if you are not a linguist, you can see from the above that the word "baptize" is not really a TRANSLATION of "baptizo" at all. The translators simply replaced the "o" with an "e." This is called a TRANSLITERATION not a translation, because in true translation work the meaning of the word is carried over from one language into another. In the case of the word "baptize" or "baptism" this was not done.

The result of this is that every time someone reads or hears about baptism, he automatically thinks it must mean WATER baptism. So, when such a person reads in Acts 2:38, for instance, "Repent and be baptized... for the remission of sins," he erroneously concludes that one must be dipped in water to be saved... because the verse does say you have to be baptized to receive God's forgiveness. Much harm and confusion has resulted from not understanding the real meaning of baptism. It means "to whelm (engulf or cover) and to cleanse." When Scripture refers to WATER baptism the context ALWAYS makes this clear. When water is not mentioned in connection with baptism, we need to use utmost care in our study of the passage so that we will recognize what kind of "baptism" (cleansing or whelming) is being spoken of.

KINDS OF BAPTISMS IN SCRIPTURE

There are at least six different kinds of baptisms spoken of in the Bible:

(1) The baptism of John (Matthew 21:25),
(2) The baptism of repentance (Mark 1:4),
(3) Baptism or cleansing into death (Romans 6:4),
(4) Baptism in water (Matthew 3:11),
(5) Baptism in the Spirit (Matthew 3:11; I Corinthians 12:13), and
(6) Baptism unto Moses (I Corinthians 10:2).

The above is sufficient to cause us to think twice before assuming that baptism must always refer to water.

THE BAPTISM NECESSARY FOR SALVATION

Mark 16:16 says, "He that believeth and is baptized shall be saved; but he that believeth not shall be damned." Obviously, therefore, there is a baptism that is necessary for salvation. We cannot assume, however, that this refers to WATER baptism. Scripture clearly tells us what kind of baptism it is that is necessary for salvation.

John the Baptist, differentiating between his baptism and Christ's baptism, said, "I indeed have baptized you with WATER: but He (Christ) shall baptize you with the HOLY GHOST" (Mark 1:8). After Christ's death, burial, and resurrection, Paul came upon some of John's disciples who were not saved, even though they had been baptized by John in water. They had not as yet received the baptism (cleansing) of the Holy Spirit. When they did, they were saved (Acts 19:1-7; compare with Romans 8:9). It is the SPIRIT'S baptism that is essential for salvation... not WATER baptism.

The Lord Jesus Christ never baptized anyone with water the whole time He was on earth. If water baptism were necessary for salvation, then Christ would have been withholding salvation from everyone He dealt with.

Ephesians 4:5 says that there is "one baptism" which God recognizes today. And I Corinthians 12:13 describes it clearly: "For by one SPIRIT are we all (no believers excluded) baptized into one body... and have been all made to drink into one SPIRIT." Notice that the "one Spirit" and "one baptism" of Ephesians 4: 4, 5 parallel perfectly with the "one Spirit" and "one body" of I Corinthians 12:13. THIS is the baptism (or cleansing) necessary for salvation. This baptism is performed by God, not by man.

HOW AND WHEN THE BAPTISM OF THE SPIRIT IS RECEIVED

For you to be a child of God you must have the Holy Spirit for God says, "... Now if any man have NOT the Spirit of Christ, HE IS NONE OF HIS" (Romans 8:9). John 1:12, 13 tells us we become children of God, born of Him, WHEN we receive Christ by faith. And WHEN we receive Christ, we also receive the Spirit.

"And in Him you Gentiles also, after listening to the message of the truth, the good news of your salvation-having believed in Him-were sealed with the promised Holy Spirit..." (Eph. 1:13, Weymouth trans., 3rd ed.).

Jesus said in John 7:39, "But this spake He of the Spirit, which they that believe on Him should receive...." The Holy Spirit is given to believers at the moment of salvation, and He indwells them forever.

"What? Know ye not that your body is the temple of the Holy Ghost, which is in you, which ye have of God, and ye are not your own?" (I Cor. 6:19) The letter of I Corinthians was written to ALL believers (1:2), so then, ALL BELIEVERS are indwelt by the Spirit and have received His baptism or cleansing.

Passages Some People Think Teach Water Baptism for Salvation

Acts 2:38, "Then Peter said unto them, Repent, and be baptized every one of you in the Name of Jesus Christ for the remission of sins, and ye shall receive the gift of the Holy Ghost." You will discover what this verse means if you keep these important things clear in your mind:

(1) To be "baptized" means to be "cleansed."

(2) These unbelieving Jews were pricked in their hearts when Peter reminded them that they had a part in crucifying Jesus. And Peter tells them to be CLEANSED of this sin "IN the NAME of Jesus Christ"-the very One they helped crucify.

(3) Peter said to be "baptized in the Name of Jesus Christ." Some assume that Peter meant for these people to be baptized in water, and as they were being baptized, Peter would say over them, "I baptize you in the Name of Jesus Christ." However, this is not what God has recorded. It is what men have added. GOD says these people were cleansed in CHRIST'S NAME. Remember, His Name means "God who saves, keeps, satisfies," etc. There is cleansing power in His Name!

(4) Notice, when these people were cleansed in Christ, they received the gift of the Holy Spirit. Therefore, this is another verse showing that the baptism or cleansing that accompanies salvation is of the Spirit -not of water.

(5) Notice, it says the GIFT of the Holy Spirit. If you needed water baptism for salvation or to receive the Holy Spirit, neither salvation nor the Holy Spirit would be a GIFT of God, but of the works of man.

(6) When "baptism" refers to water, it means to be made fully wet; when it refers to salvation, it means to be fully or completely cleansed by the Spirit. Acts 2:41 records that 3,000 trusted Christ as the result of Peter's message. If the baptism here were referring to WATER baptism, where could Peter baptize 3,000 people? He and all the people were in the Temple area, and there was NO WATER THERE except for a small laver in which the priests washed their hands and feet before entering into the Holy Place. But verse 41 says that these 3,000 souls were added to the disciples that "same day." In the entire passage water is not mentioned even once.

Literally translated, Acts 2:3 8 could read, "Then Peter said unto them, Change your mind, and be CLEANSED every one of you in the Name of Jesus Christ for the forgiveness of sins, and ye shall receive the gift of the Holy Ghost." Mark 16:16, "He that believeth and is baptized shall be saved; but he that believeth not shall be damned." Please notice four things about this verse:

(1) Only unbelief condemns. Being water baptized or not being water baptized has nothing to do with it.

(2) The baptism here is Spirit baptism, not water baptism.

(3) He that believeth and is cleansed shall be saved. We do the believing, and God does the cleansing. "And such were some of you: but ye are washed; but ye are sanctified; but ye are justified in the Name of the Lord Jesus, and by the Spirit of our God" (I Cor. 6:11).

(4) The passage in Mark 16, "from verse 9 to the end (of the chapter) is not found in the two most ancient manuscripts, the Sinaitic and Vatican, and others have it with partial omissions and variations. But it is quoted by Irenaeus and Hippolytus in the second or third century" (Scofield's note 1, by Mark 16:9).

John 3:5, "Jesus answered, Verily, verily, I say unto thee, Except a man be born of water and of the Spirit, he cannot enter into the kingdom of God."

Some people think this verse is referring to water baptism because it says you must be "born of water." But let me ask you a question. Are BIRTH and BAPTISM the same thing? Of course not! If Christ wanted to say, "You must be baptized of water," He would have said so. But He said, "born of water," and Jesus knew the difference between the two.

Consider the context. The first time Jesus told Nicodemus of the new birth, He said, "Except a man be BORN again, he cannot see the kingdom of God" (verse 3). Nicodemus thought Christ's statement was referring to another physical birth. In fact, he asked, "How can a man be born when he is old? Can he enter the second time into his mother's womb, and be born?" (verse 4)

We KNOW that the BIRTH OF WATER in John 3:5 cannot mean water baptism. There are at least three things this could mean within the context and without contradicting other parts of the Word of God:

(1) Some Bible scholars believe that being "born of water" refers to physical birth. Notice Christ's reply to Nicodemus that a man has to be BORN (the subject throughout is BIRTH, not baptism) of water and the Spirit. Christ was saying, "Nicodemus, you must be born of water (physical birth) and the Spirit (new birth)." Why is it said that being "born of water" refers to physical birth? Because of Christ's clear explanation in the very next verse, "That which is born of the FLESH is flesh; and that which is born of the SPIRIT is Spirit" (v.6). Jesus then said, "Marvel not (don't be surprised) that I said unto thee, "Ye must be BORN again."

(2) Other Bible scholars believe that being "born of water" refers to the Holy Spirit. Throughout the Gospel of John water is used as an illustration to point to Christ as the giver of "living water," as in John 4:6-14. Christ asked the woman at Jacob's well for a drink of water and also told the woman that He could give her water as well.... But the water He gives is not "H20".... The water that He gives is a "well of water springing up into everlasting life" (v. 14). In John 7:39 Christ gave this explanation of "living water": "But this spake He of the Spirit which they that believe on Him should receive...."

The Greek word for "and" in John 3:5 is "kai." Quoting from Strong's Concordance, #2532, we find that this word is a "primitive participle, having a copulative (joining together) and sometimes also a cumulative force." Besides being translated "and" it is also translated "indeed, likewise, moreover," etc.

To paraphrase John 3:5, then, it could read, "... except a man be born of water (the living water Christ gives), indeed, by the Spirit, he cannot enter into the kingdom of God."

(3) Still other Bible scholars believe the birth of water in John 3:5 is speaking of the "washing of the Word" as is mentioned in Ephesians 5:26 and Titus 3:5.

The important thing for us to know is that salvation is always and only by faith in the Lord Jesus Christ, and this passage in John 3:5 in no way suggests water baptism for salvation.

For someone to conclude that John 3:5 is referring to WATER BAPTISM, he would have to ignore completely the entire context of the third chapter.

I Peter 3:21, "The like figure whereunto even baptism doth also now save us (not the putting away of the filth of the flesh, but the answer of a good conscience toward God) by the resurrection of Jesus Christ."

This verse isn't even speaking of salvation of a person's soul, but of being saved or delivered from a guilty conscience of not obeying God. (In this case, obeying God by being water baptized AFTER salvation!)

However, those who believe water baptism is essential for salvation often use this verse, so we will go into some detail on its explanation. (But in all the times this verse has been used, I have never yet had a single person quote more than the first part of the verse-"The like figure whereunto even baptism doth also now save us....")

It is as if Satan has put blinders on these people, for they fail to see that the verse goes on to state clearly that this salvation is not a salvation which in any way puts "away the sins of the flesh." Notice how emphatic the Lord is: "NOT the putting away of the filth of the flesh...." Yet time and time again when I have pointed this out to those who think this verse teaches baptismal regeneration, they act as if they had never seen the last part of the verse before. But the Lord put it there to keep us from being confused.

But someone will say, "The verse does say 'baptism doth also now save us.'" Yes, it does, and the Word of God tells us what it saves us from.

The verse itself, with the context, answers the question, "what does baptism save us from?" Verse 20 says that "eight souls (Noah and his family) were saved by water." The word "by" literally should read "through" the water. You can check this yourself in any number of other good translations-American Standard Version, Williams, Weymouth, New English Bible, etc.

It is certainly clear when you read of the flood in Genesis, chapter seven, that people were not saved BY the water. They were condemned and killed BY the water. But the eight believers who were in the ARK (a type of being in CHRIST) were saved THROUGH the water, by the ark. Literally, verse 20 reads "eight souls were saved through the water."

When verse 21 says, "baptism doth also now save us," we need to understand that there are different kinds of "salvation" just as there are different kinds of "baptisms."

Some examples of different kinds of salvation in Scripture are:

James 5:15, "the prayer of faith shall save (protect, deliver) the sick, and the Lord shall raise him up...." Here it is not speaking of salvation of the soul, but deliverance from physical illness.

Acts 27:31, "Except these abide in the ship, ye cannot be saved." Saved from what? Saved from drowning. Suppose I began a new cult. I might call it the "Shipites," and I could use this verse as my divinely given authority that people had to live in ships to be saved. But how many people do you think would be saved if you had to live in ships for salvation?

Hebrews 5:7 mentions that the Father was able to save (or deliver) Jesus from physical death. But Jesus gave His life voluntarily (John 10:18), and even though He knew He would suffer in the flesh, He endured the cross for the joy of seeing souls saved through His payment for their sin.

The Greek word in I Peter 3:21, and elsewhere in the Bible, translated "save" is "sozo" and means "to be saved, protected, or delivered." You must always read the context to see what kind of protection, or deliverance, or salvation is being spoken of.

I Peter 3:21 is clear as to what kind of salvation and deliverance is meant here. Notice the words carefully: "baptism doth also now save (protect, deliver) us (NOT the putting away of the filth of the flesh, but the answer of a good conscience toward God)...." As children of God by faith, we should follow Christ's command to be water baptized after we are saved, and when we obey this command we have a clear conscience. We are delivered from a conscience which condemns us (Matt. 28:19; Acts 8:36-38; Acts 10: 47, 48).

In I Cor. 1:17 Paul said, "For Christ sent me not to baptize, but to preach the gospel...." If water baptism were necessary for salvation, then Paul, in effect, would be saying, "For Christ sent me not to see that people were saved, but to preach the gospel...." Anyone can see how ludicrous this would be. In I Cor. 1:14 Paul would have been saying, "I thank God that none of you were saved, but Crispus and Gaius." This would completely nullify the entire purpose of Paul's whole ministry.

Water baptism NEVER cleanses or washes away sin. ONLY CHRIST'S BLOOD can do that (Ephesians 1:7). Salvation comes through our faith.

The ordinance of communion is a type of our salvation by the death of Christ. The ordinance of baptism is a type of our service by the power of the Holy Spirit.

Service comes through our obedience, and as believers we should obey God's Word, following His commands to the best of our ability. In this obedience, water baptism should certainly be included. It is a testimony to others that we are now walking in newness of life (Romans 6:4).

How to Witness to Those Who Believe in Water Baptism for Salvation

(1) As is true in most witnessing situations, the issue is "grace versus works" (water baptism). Use Ephesians 2: 8, 9 or Romans 4:5.

(2) Instead of arguing over "baptism" passages, give the plan of salvation, emphasizing clear salvation verses like John 6:47. It is necessary to interpret unclear verses by clear verses, and never the other way around.

(3) Ask questions about the salvation verses so the meaning will become crystal clear to the person. For instance: "Who has everlasting life, according to John 6:47?" Answer: "He who BELIEVES on Christ." Question: "Well, if you HAVE everlasting life by trusting in Christ as your Saviour, what more do you need?" Answer: "Nothing!"

Water baptism doesn't help you to get saved. It has nothing to do with your salvation.

(4) Often people who believe in water baptism for salvation also think other "works" are necessary for salvation as well. They say there are other conditions for salvation besides belief, and you have to read the entire Bible to find out what they are. To answer this type of objection, simply turn to Bible examples where unbelievers were told exactly what to do to be saved: Christ told Nicodemus just to believe and receive everlasting life (John 3:16-18). Paul told the Philippian jailor just to believe and be saved (Acts 16:30, 31). Paul told the Jews just to believe and receive forgiveness of all sin (Acts 13:26, 38, 39).

None of these people mentioned above had the whole Bible to go through. They wanted to be saved then and there (especially the Philippian jailor who was about to commit suicide). Do you think Paul or Jesus told them only PART of what they had to do to be saved? Half a truth, in this case especially, would certainly be a lie! Would you, yourself, be that careless and heartless? What could be more clear than "Believe on the Lord Jesus Christ and thou SHALT BE SAVED!"

The thief on the cross didn't come down and get water baptized, but he went to heaven. (Heaven and paradise are the same place according to II Cor. 12:1-4). Paul thanked God that he didn't baptize very many people (I Cor. 1:11 21). If water baptism were necessary for salvation, then Paul would be thanking God he didn't see that many were saved! Unthinkable!

Not only that, but Christ never baptized anyone with water. If water baptism were necessary for salvation, then Christ withheld from those He dealt with, salvation. But He came to "seek and to SAVE!"

CHAPTER X – Evolution

To cover exhaustively the subject of evolution and creation would obviously require much more information than we can include in one chapter, but this is written to help you get some idea of how you could answer a lost person if he should offer his belief in evolution as an excuse not to receive Christ as his Saviour.

For further information on evolution you might want to read some of the books recommended in Chapter 22. Winning an argument on evolution might make you feel brilliant, but remember that if your presentation aggravates the lost person, you run the risk of his not trusting Christ because he got mad from losing an argument.

If you can answer the person's questions on evolution simply and quickly and go immediately back to the plan of salvation, you will accomplish much more than if you spend hours in needless arguing. Your scientific knowledge is not the power of God unto salvation, even when you are witnessing to a person who is interested in science-it is still the gospel that is the power of God unto his salvation. Wisely keep this in mind.

Definitions

Materialistic Evolution: Existence and progression of life without help from God.

Theistic Evolution: Progression of life from some primitive form which God might have created, but which evolved without the help of God from the first form of life onward.

The Biblical Doctrine: God created everything. "ALL things were made by Him, and without Him was not ANY thing made that was made" (John 1:3).

At the end of the chapter we will give many verses in the Word of God which expressly teach creation.

Below is information of which, if you know, you can briefly present one or two things, and perhaps be able to turn the conversation back to the gospel quickly, without getting into a big discussion with the person and having him "lose face." This is your aim.

Fact or Theory?

Evolution, transmutation of species, has never been proven. The reason for this is very simple. It has never happened! Evolution is no more than the imaginations of men who deny the Word of God and so are desperately struggling for some explanation of the origin of life. It is here. Somehow it got here. God says He created it. Those who do not accept God's Word must seek some other explanation. The evolutionist is trying hard. But somehow he isn't getting anywhere.

Even Charles Darwin himself, recognizing that although there is mutation within the species, there are no transmutations-no changes from one species (or family) into an other, wrote in his book, My Life and Letters, Volume One, Page 210, "Not one change of species into another is on record. We cannot prove that a single species has been changed (into another)."

The Missing Link

The great search for the "missing link" points out the error of the theory of evolution more emphatically than anything I know of. Now think this through. Here we are, completely developed human beings. Evolutionists teach that the closest animal down the ladder from man probably is the ape, the gorilla, or some similar, if yet unidentified, animal. Their theories on what animal this is change from time to time. Whichever animal they think would be closest to the human being-they are trying to find a "missing link" from it to man.

But if evolution were true, there would be no need to SEARCH for a "missing link" because there would be SO MANY MORE "in-betweens" than there are terminals, since the fully developed man would be a result of many years of small changes from (let us say, for the sake of this illustration) the ape to the man.

Archeologists would constantly be digging up skeletons, millions and millions of them, part man and part ape. There would have to be skeletons of ALL the various stages of development from ape to man. But WHERE ARE THESE MILLIONS OF SKELETONS? Why is anyone looking for a "missing link" anyway? The whole CHAIN of missing links is missing!

Original Matter

Probably the biggest problem, because it is certainly insurmountable, to the materialistic evolutionist is: Who or what is responsible for the FIRST piece of matter?

Regardless of their particular theory of HOW the world was formed, they cannot deny it has been formed, and they cannot tell where the first matter CAME FROM, which was used in making the world.

In Jeremiah 10:12 God tells us what He used to create the earth. He used His power (in the Hebrew, His "energy"). It is interesting to note that in our own lifetime Albert Einstein formulated the Relativity Equation, $E=MC^2$, which is exactly what God said in the Bible 2,600 years ago.

Simply put, his formula states that matter and energy are equivalent. One can obtain energy (E) equal to the quantity of matter (M) multiplied by the square of the speed of light (C) (186,000 miles per second). God told us, long before the scientific world recognized it, that matter was created out of energy.

Evolutionists would like to make those who believe the Bible feel ignorant for believing so in this age of knowledge. But anyone who thinks the Bible disagrees with science either doesn't know the Bible very well or isn't speaking of real science.

God says of the men in this age of knowledge who deny His Word, that they are "Ever learning, and never able to come to the knowledge of the truth" (II Tim. 3:7).

Since they will not accept God's explanation of the origin of the earth, they must try to find some sort of reasonable explanation on their own. Sorry, but evolution isn't it. It isn't reasonable, and it isn't even POSSIBLE.

Second Law of Thermodynamics

Quoting from the book, Evolution and Human Destiny, by Kohler, "One of the most fundamental maxims of the physical sciences is the trend toward greater randomness- the fact that, on the average, things will get into disorder rather than into order, if left to themselves. This is essentially the statement that is embodied in the Second Law of Thermodynamics." This scientific law actually refutes and contradicts the theory of evolution in its entirety. The whole universe is NOT getting better and more specialized; it is running down; it is wearing out.

"Ladder of Creation"

Many evolutionists teach that the following, in order, evolved upward from the beginning: atom, molecule, protein molecule, virus, bacteria, algae, protozoa, metazoa, man. This cannot be true. The protein molecule couldn't develop from just atoms and molecules, unless protein, were already present. Man has been trying to create protein from various chemicals and compounds and has been unsuccessful. Only God can create protein.

The virus could not exist before higher life than the virus had been created because the virus requires a "host cell" to live off of. A virus cannot live off of just atoms, molecules, and protein molecules. So, you see, the "ladder of creation," created by the evolutionists to prove their theory, actually in itself disproves the theory of evolution.

Fixity of Species

When your dog is going to have a litter, don't worry that she will have a litter of monkeys instead of a litter of puppies. That she will have puppies was determined when her chromosomes joined with her mate's chromosomes at conception.

You see, a dog has only 22 chromosomes, whereas a monkey has 54. Half the total number of chromosomes are contained in the female reproductive cells and half are contained in the male. So the exact total number are brought together in the offspring.

Man has 46 chromosomes. This chromosome count is a steady factor. This determines what is called the "fixity of species" because the chromosome count doesn't vary. People always give birth to people. Dogs always give birth to dogs, etc.

It is the genes that produce variety within the species. Genes allow for people to be short, tall, fat, thin, blond, brunette, etc., but still all PEOPLE.

The chromosomes make crossing of the species an uncrossable barrier. This certainly would hinder any evolution. It would stop it dead in its tracks!

The Horse

A standard "demonstration" of evolutionists has been the horse, the "EOHIPPUS." They give a long list for the supposed evolution of the horse, as follows:

Eohippus
Orohippus
Epihippus
Mesohippus
Miohippus
Anchiterium

Hypohippus
Parahippus
Merychippus
Hipparion
Protohippus
Pliophippus
Genus Equus

What the evolutionists do not tell you is that fossils of the little Eohippus rodent and fossils of the Equus Nevadensis and Equus Occidentalis (fully developed horses as we know them today) are contemporary. They are found in the same "geological age" strata.

Why try to manufacture some "evolution" of the horse when you already have a horse?

Fossils

What does the record in the rocks show us? The record in the rocks and the record in the Bible agree perfectly. When life is found, all forms of life are found. When a family appears, it is completely and fully developed. No fossils of "in-betweens" are ever found. There aren't any. This must really mystify those who accept the theory of evolution.

"Onion Skin" Theory

Most evolutionists teach that the earth is layered into many strata, and that in each stratum, starting with the deepest and going up to the top layers, are the remains of different forms of life in the order of progressive evolution. This is not true. There is not one place on earth where more than four strata occur, and in each stratum all kinds of life are found, and not in the order the evolutionists would have us believe.

The "ages" that the evolutionists teach that different stages of life have been found within are (1) Azoic (without life), (2) Archeozoic (beginning life), (3) Proterozoic (early life), (4) Paleozoic (old, ancient life), (5) Mesozoic (middle life), and (6) Cenozoic (new, recent life). Within the Cenozoic age is another group of ages called the "cenes": Paleocene, Eocene, Oligocene, Pliocene, and Pleistocene (recent, old life; dawn life; less recent life; more recent life; and most recent, human life-respectively).

The supposed times of these "ages" differ from one evolutionist to the next, some teaching that in the Archeozoic age of beginning life fossils date back to one billion years ago.

Nature's Balance

God has so arranged His creation that there is a delicate balance in nature which serves to maintain everything in its proper relationship, and without which the earth would be complete chaos.

For instance, animals take in oxygen and give off carbon dioxide. Plants take in carbon dioxide and give off oxygen. Plants could not live without animals, and neither could animals live without plants. But evolutionists teach plants evolved LONG before animals came upon the scene. This is impossible.

Another balance is that plants give off alkali and animals give off acid. Without plants the world would be too acid. They need each other to maintain conditions suitable for one another.

Ontogeny Recapitulates Phylogeny

This is the theory that the human fetus in the mother's womb goes through all the phases of the evolutionary process. Evolutionists capitalize on things like the structure in the embryo which RESEMBLES gill slits of fish in APPEARANCE, saying that the embryo is now going through this particular stage of evolution.

A scientist should know that RESEMBLANCE of APPEARANCE does not in any way prove RELATIONSHIP in fact. My fountain pen and the fountain pen of an "Undercover Agent" might resemble each other in appearance, but his pen is really a radio transmitter and receiver.

The human embryo doesn't go through any stages of evolution.

THE FIRST SEX

Simple forms of life reproduce by "mitosis," which is cell division. The cell splits, and then there are two. The result is two of whatever you had one of before-just one more of the same thing, not a step up some "evolutionary scale."

Let me ask you a question. If evolution were true, when would life have gotten tired of reproducing by mitosis and desired to reproduce by another means, by sex? One "glob" would have to say to another "glob," "Let's change our way of reproduction. I'm tired of doing it the same old way. I'll develop into a male, and you develop into a female."

But before they could ever reproduce, they would have to develop the reproductive organs completely and perfectly, or they would not function. Sometimes I wonder if the evolutionist stops to realize how complicated the reproductive organs are. If there is just one tiny thing wrong, reproduction is hindered.

Before that first enterprising "glob couple" could have ever developed functioning reproductive organs, they would have been long dead and gone. Did that "glob couple" THINK out the problems and TELL another "glob couple" to carry out their project?

THE EYE

Evolutionists cannot conceive how the human's intricate eyes ever evolved. It is a tremendously delicate, complex organ. They say perhaps the eye developed from some light-sensitive spot like a freckle.

Personally, it taxes my imagination and challenges my intelligence much less to accept the fact that God CREATED us with all our faculties than to try to believe the theory that the human eye evolved from some freckle. An ophthalmologist must spend many years in specialized study after college even to understand the eye well enough to treat it. How could something without even human intelligence actually design and put together the human eye? It would be impossible!

The eye certainly had to be CREATED BY GOD. "I will praise Thee; for I am fearfully and wonderfully made: marvelous are Thy works; and that my soul knoweth right well" (Psalm 139:14).

THE "GAP" THEORY

Genesis 1:2, in the King James, reads, "And the earth was without form, and void; and darkness was upon the face of the deep...."

The word "was" should properly be translated "became," as we see from the oldest manuscripts below:

(1) Chaldee-became desert and empty.
(2) Septuagint-became unfurnished and empty.
(3) Aramaic-became ruined and uninhabited.
(4) Vulgate-became dreary and empty.

Genesis 1:1 says "In the beginning God created the heaven and the earth." THERE IS A TIME LAPSE, A GAP, between the events in Gen. 1:1 and Gen. 1:2. There could be millions of years between the two verses. No one knows for how many years the earth was laid waste. We do know from Isaiah 45:18 that God did not create the earth in a state of waste to begin with. "For thus saith the LORD that created the heavens; God himself that formed the earth and made it, he hath established it, he created it NOT IN VAIN, he formed it to be inhabited...."

We believe that after the fall of Satan God judged the earth, and at that time the earth became ruined. God made it desolate after previous life. In the time of Genesis 1:1, and before the time of Genesis 1:2, any of the true historical ages and the true ancient fossils would fit. The Bible does NOT say that the earth is only 6,000 years old. The Bible does not date the original creation spoken of in Genesis 1:1.

The Bible Says God Created Plants

Genesis 1:29, "And God said, Behold, I have given you every herb bearing seed, which is upon the... earth, and every tree, in the which is the fruit of a tree yielding seed; to you it shall be for meat."

Isaiah 41:19, 20, "I will plant in the wilderness the cedar, the shittah tree, and the myrtle, and the oil tree; I will set in the desert the fir tree, and the pine, and the box tree together; That they may see and know and consider, and understand together, that the hand of the Lord hath done this, and the Holy One of Israel hath CREATED it."

God Created Animals

Genesis 1: 24, 25, "And God said, Let the earth bring forth the living creature after his kind, cattle, and creeping thing, and beast of the earth after his kind: and it was so. And GOD made the beast of the earth after his kind, and cattle after their kind, and everything that creepeth upon the earth after his kind: and God saw that it was good."

I Cor. 15:38, 39, "But GOD giveth it a body as it hath pleased Him, and to every seed his own body. All flesh is NOT the same flesh: but there is one kind of flesh of men, another flesh of beasts, another of fishes, and another of birds."

Psalm 32:9, "Be ye not as the horse, or as the mule, which have no understanding...." Animals do not have a spirit. They do not have mental discernment. They could not decide to better themselves via "evolution."

Psalm 36:6, "... O Lord, Thou preservest man and beast." Notice, it is not the "survival of the fittest." It is God who preserves.

God Created Man

Genesis 2:7, "And the LORD GOD formed man of the dust of the ground, and breathed into his nostrils the breath of life; and man became a living soul." (Prof. E. Slossen, analytical chemist in Washington, D.C., proved that the dust of the ground contains 14 elements and that man's body contains the exact same 14 elements.)

Job 20:4, "Knowest thou not this of old, since man was PLACED upon the earth?" Man didn't arrive through evolution. He was placed!

Job 32:8, "But there is a spirit in man: and the inspiration of the Almighty giveth them understanding." Notice the contrast between man in this verse and animals in Psalm 32:9. God made the difference from the beginning. Man didn't somewhere along the way "pick up" a spirit!

Job 33:4, "The SPIRIT OF GOD hath MADE me, and the breath of the Almighty hath given me life."

Psalm 100:3, "Know ye that the Lord He is GOD: it is HE that hath MADE us, and not we ourselves...."

Romans 9:20, "Nay but, O man, who art thou that repliest against God? Shall the thing formed say to HIM that formed it, Why hast Thou made me thus?"

Isaiah 43:7, "Even every one that is called by My Name: for I have created him for My glory, I have FORMED him; yea; I have MADE him."

Isaiah 45:12, "I have MADE the earth, and CREATED MAN upon it: I, even My hands,. have stretched out the heavens, and all their hosts have I commanded."

Psalm 95:6, "O come, let us worship and bow down: let us kneel before the LORD our MAKER."

God Created Heaven and Earth

Genesis 1: 1, "In the beginning God created the heaven and the earth."

Romans 1:20, "For the invisible things of Him from the CREATION of the world are clearly seen, being understood by the things that are made, even His eternal power and Godhead; so that they are without excuse."

John 1:10, "He was in the world, and the world was MADE by Him, and the world knew Him not." Isaiah 45:18, "For thus saith the Lord that CREATED the heavens; God Himself that FORMED the earth and MADE it; He hath established it; He created it not in vain, He formed it to be inhabited: I am the Lord, and there is none else."

God Created Everything

Hebrews 3:4, "For every house is builded by some man; but He that built all things is God."

Colossians 1:16, "For by Him were ALL THINGS CREATED, that are in heaven, and that are in earth, visible and invisible, whether they be thrones, or dominions, or principalities, or powers: ALL THINGS WERE CREATED BY HIM, and for Him."

Acts 17:24, "God that made the world and ALL THINGS therein, seeing that He is Lord of heaven and earth, dwelleth not in temples made with hands."

Revelation 4:11, "Thou art worthy, O Lord, to receive glory and honour and power, for Thou hast CREATED ALL THINGS, and for Thy pleasure they are and were created."

Revelation 10:6, "And sware by Him that liveth for ever and ever, who CREATED heaven, and the things that therein are, and the earth, and the things that therein are, and the sea, and the things which are therein, that there should be time no longer."

Acts 4:24, "And when they heard that, they lifted up their voice to God with one accord, and said, Lord, Thou art God, which hast made heaven, and earth, and the sea, and ALL that in them is."

In Conclusion

Science cannot prove evolution because it is not a fact. The Bible clearly teaches creation as you have just read. Please remember as you witness to a lost person, if the subject of evolution should come up, to answer it as quickly as possible and get back to the plan of salvation.

CHAPTER XI—The Atheist and Agnostic

Often a person is an atheist or skeptic because he has observed the many inconsistencies in the various Christian denominations.

Things like the dark ages, the "holy" wars of the Crusades, the superstition and anti-intellectual climate that have surrounded much of Christendom, the critical attitudes of pseudo-pious people who consider themselves Christians, have all played a part in abetting skepticism and unbelief.

Therefore, when you witness to a skeptical person, you will often find that you can agree with many things he is unhappy about in the organized religions he is rejecting.

It is important to be kind, courteous, and in every way maintain high standards as you deal with skeptics, because naturally they will be looking for any reason they can find to uphold their disregard for Christianity. Let them see that a person who has really accepted Christ as his Saviour is NOT a hypocrite but is a person who is sincerely trying to live a life that is honest before God and man... not, of course, to be saved, but because he is saved.

God

"The fool said in his heart, there is no God" (Psalm 14:1). More people will fit into the category of an agnostic than that of an atheist. While the atheist has convinced himself that there is no God, the agnostic doesn't know if there is a God and doesn't know if anyone can really know there is a God. Many college students today wonder about the existence and reality of a personal God.

These people need to see that we don't believe in God just because our parents do, our church does, or because it is "nice" to believe in God, but because we are convinced God is real, alive, and vitally interested in us.

Below are reasons we believe in God:

1. Creation requires a Creator. The owner of a wrist watch knows there was a creator of that wrist watch. Intelligence, thought, and effort were required to make the watch.

Our magnificent bodies, our complex world, our immense, orderly universe, are all evidences of a Creator. It took intelligence, thought, and effort to make us and the world we find ourselves in.

There are LAWS governing our universe-laws of gravity, motion, seasons, tides, wind circuits, etc. These laws presuppose a LawGIVER. Our universe has design and had to have a Designer.

2. The Bible had to be written by God. Further in this chapter we shall mention reasons why we know the Bible is the Word of God. It is impossible for the Bible to have been written by man alone. The very fact that the Bible is written as it is proves that there had to have been a higher intelligence guiding the writers. Because we know there is a God, we can see the logic and reasonableness of God's writing the Bible. But conversely, because we know the Bible, we can prove there is a God who wrote it.

3. A person who doesn't believe in God will have to face the problem of trying to substantiate a negative. This particular negative would be impossible to prove. Here is why.

How can a person prove there is no God? Has this person been everywhere within and without the universe? If there is somewhere he has not been, God might be there. Does this person know everything? If there is something he does not know, that something might be God.

4. Thousands of Christians testify that they know God, that they talk to God, and He hears their prayers and proves it by ANSWERING their prayers.

Usually the person who is atheistic or agnostic also tends to feel that he is scientific. To such a person you might point out that no true scientist would reject the testimony of thousands of people that a certain Person exists, has the highest form of intelligence and personality, and loves people tremendously. Certainly, such marvelous claims compel the HONEST skeptic to make a thorough investigation into the matter and not to come to any hasty conclusion that there is no God.

It has been said that when it comes to God and the Bible, an honest skeptic will not be a skeptic very long because after investigation into the matter he will no longer be a skeptic.

To those who don't believe in God or who think God is dead, let me say, "My God is alive! Sorry about yours!"

The Bible

If a person says he doesn't believe the Bible, tell him the gospel before proving the Bible is God's Word. Maybe he doesn't believe the Bible because he doesn't understand the plan of salvation and thinks he will be sent to hell because of his bad life. If this is the case, you probably could lead him to the Lord without ever having to go into why you know the Bible is the Word of God.

Reasons for Believing the Bible

1. The men who wrote the Bible testify that God gave them the words to write. "The word that came to Jeremiah FROM THE LORD, saying, Thus speaketh THE LORD GOD of Israel, WRITE thee all the words that I HAVE SPOKEN UNTO THEE IN A BOOK.... And these are the words that the Lord spake..." (Jer. 30:1, 2, 4).

"The WORD OF THE LORD came expressly unto Ezekiel the priest..." (Ezekiel 1:3).

If the men who wrote the Bible hadn't been inspired of God, they certainly would have recanted under the great persecution they received. Men are not willing to die for something which they know to be untrue.

2. John Wesley, the founder of the Methodist denomination, said something like this: The Bible was written either by-

(a) good men,
(b) bad men, or
(c) God.

(a) If good men wrote the Bible and then claimed it was written by the inspiration of God, they would be liars, and liars are not good men. They would be deceivers, and good men don't purposely deceive people.
(b) If bad men wrote the Bible, they would be condemning themselves because the Bible condemns sin. Bad men tend to justify themselves, but the Bible never justifies sin. Bad men couldn't have written the Bible because the Bible is a good book.
(c) Since neither good men nor bad men wrote the Bible, the only person left is God. God wrote the Bible, and it is a MASTERPIECE OF HIS HANDIWORK!

3. The Bible contains true prophecy... history written before it happens!... and so much of it that this is one of the biggest proofs that the Bible was written by God, who knows the future (and not by man, who doesn't know the future). Below are verses telling us how to tell the difference between false and true prophecy.

Deut. 18:21, 22, "And if thou say in thine heart, How shall we know the word which the Lord hath NOT spoken? When a prophet speaketh in the Name of the Lord, if the thing FOLLOW NOT, NOR COME TO PASS, that is the thing which the Lord hath NOT spoken, but the prophet hath spoken it presumptuously: thou shalt not be afraid of him."

Ezek. 12:25, "For I am the Lord: I will speak, and the word that I shall speak SHALL COME TO PASS"

Jer. 23:25-32, "I have heard what the prophets said, that prophesy LIES in my name, saying, I have dreamed, I have dreamed. How long shall this be in the heart of the prophets that prophesy lies? Yea, they are prophets of the DECEIT OF THEIR OWN HEART, which think to cause My people to forget My Name by their dreams which they tell every man to his neighbor, as their fathers have forgotten My Name for Baal.

"The prophet that hath a dream, let him tell a dream; and he that hath My Word, let him speak My Word faithfully. What is the chaff to the wheat? saith the Lord. Is not My Word like as a fire? saith the Lord; and like a hammer that breaketh the rock in pieces? Therefore, behold, I am against the prophets saith the Lord, that steal My Words everyone from his neighbor. "Behold, I am against the prophets, saith the Lord, that use their tongues, and say, HE saith. Behold, I am against them that prophesy false dreams, saith the Lord, and do tell them, and cause My people to err by their lies, and by their lightness; yet I SENT THEM NOT, nor commanded them: therefore, they shall not profit this people at all, saith the Lord."

Isaiah 46:9, 10, "Remember the former things of old: for I am God, and there is none else; I am God, and there is none like Me, declaring the END from the BEGINNING, and from ancient times the things that are NOT YET DONE, saying, My counsel SHALL STAND, and I WILL DO all My pleasure."

John 14:29, "And now I have told you BEFORE it come to pass, that WHEN IT IS COME TO PASS, ye might believe."

Isaiah 48: 3-5, "I have declared the former things from the beginning; and they went forth out of my mouth, and I SHEWED THEM: I DID THEM suddenly, and THEY CAME TO PASS. Because I knew that thou art obstinate, and thy neck is an iron sinew, and thy brow brass, I have even FROM THE BEGINNING declared it to thee; BEFORE IT CAME TO PASS, I shewed it thee; lest thou shouldest say, Mine idol hath done them, and my graven image, and my molten image, hath commanded them."

Isaiah 41: 22, 23 , "Let them bring forth, and shew us what SHALL HAPPEN: let them shew the former things, what they be, that we may consider them, and know the latter end of them; or declare us things FOR TO COME. Shew the things that are TO COME HEREAFTER, that we may know that ye are gods: yea, do good, or do evil, that we may be dismayed, and behold it together."

EVERYTHING that the Bible said would happen up to this point HAS HAPPENED! History itself has already proven the Bible to be the Word of God.

4. The Bible gives a pre-written history of the Jewish nation. "Their Egyptian bondage, their conquest of Canaan, the outcome of all their wars, the division of the kingdom after the reign of Solomon, the Babylonian captivity, the partial restoration of Palestine with the rebuilding of the Temple, the destruction of Jerusalem, the world-wide dispersion, all are predicted. (See Gen. 15:13-16; Exodus, chapters 1-12; I Kings 11:30-33; Jer. 25:1-14; Daniel 9:24 27, etc.)" (57 Reasons Why We Know the Bible Is the Word of God, by Meldau, Twelfth Printing, page nine).

5. What God has left out of the Bible-the false theories and superstitions of the day-is just as much an indication of the inspiration of the Bible as what God has included in it.

For instance, Job 26:7 says, "He stretcheth out the north over the empty place, and hangeth the earth upon nothing." We know today that "gravity," a law of nature, keeps the earth suspended in space. But the people in 1500 B.C., when this statement was made, certainly didn't understand anything about gravity, and they had MANY THEORIES of what kept the earth in space. Poor Job must have had a struggle within himself, knowing that to put down a statement that says the earth was "hung upon nothing" would certainly make him the object of ridicule by his friends.

The *Hindus* said the earth was on the back of an elephant, which in turn was standing on a turtle... and that the turtle was swimming in a "cosmic sea"!

The *Egyptians* postulated that the earth was resting on top of five posts. They also thought the earth was flat (while the Bible says it is round, Isa. 40:22).

The *Greeks'* story was that a man named "Atlas" carried the earth on his back... all by himself!

What kept these myths and theories (so prevalent at the time Job wrote that the earth was hung upon nothing) out of the Bible? It was the fact that Job was writing under the inspiration of God that kept these erroneous theories out. God gave Job the courage to write as God led him. Job was faithful to the Lord even in the time of trouble (Job 1: 20-22), and God used Job in a great way.

We pray you will be faithful to the Lord and have the courage to GIVE OUT from the Bible the same, clear message God has PUT INTO it! If you ever want to be used of God in a great way, you must be faithful in giving out His message.

6. After studying
    (1) the plan of salvation,
    (2) its necessity,
    (3) its results in one's life now, and
    (4) its results in one's life in the hereafter, it surely seems to be more the way God would do things, than the way MAN would do things. The whole concept of redemption is foreign to the thinking of natural man (ICor. 1:18).

"For My thoughts are not your thoughts, neither are your ways My ways, saith the Lord. For as the heavens are higher than the earth, so are My ways HIGHER than your ways, and My thoughts than your thoughts" (Isa. 55:8, 9).

7. Consider with me the fact that the Bible is a compilation of 66 separate books, written over a period of 16 centuries, with 40 different men doing the writing, many of whom (obviously) were not contemporary and had no way of comparing what they were writing with the others. And yet these writings, so uniquely penned, fit together to form ONE BIBLE, which has ONE CENTRAL THEME, and in which ALL STATEMENTS agree perfectly without contradiction. This certainly is evidence that ONE MIND was the "logos," the Planner, the Thinker, the Designer, and the Author of these Holy pages.

Suppose you were in a journalism class of 40 students and your instructor had each person in the class write an essay which would include one or more of each of the following categories:

    poetry   science
    history   morals
    romance   man

philosophy	God
theology	death
angels	heaven
prayer	hell
discipline	prophecy, etc.
law	

Do you think if you took the finished papers and put them together, you would have one, unified, uncontradictory story, with a central purpose developed throughout... not to say anything of its being a literary MASTERPIECE and able to satisfy the needs and longings of the human hearts of every century and of every class and culture of people?

8. The Bible tells of God's Holy Spirit, and how man can receive His Holy Spirit to live within him. The Holy Spirit empowers believers to live the right kind of life. This is a miracle of God, and it really works. Christians DO have God's power in their lives. Millions of lives have been miraculously changed, and people give testimony that it was through God's Holy Spirit that the change was effected.

If the Bible were not the Word of God, then just because the Bible says there is a "Holy Spirit" and that He will in dwell believers and give them power, would not make it so.

Infidels do not claim to have power to live the right kind of life because they don't believe the Bible is the Word of God. No other book, system of theology, or philosophy can give its followers the POWER to CHANGE THEIR LIVES!

9. The Bible is scientifically accurate. While the Bible is not a book primarily concerned with science, where it does deal with science, it is completely accurate. Consider the following statements which are NOW known, but which were certainly not the opinion of such scientists as there might have been at the time they were written.

Job 26:7-Empty place in the North
Job 26:7-Earth hung upon nothing
Isa. 40:22-The earth is round
Prov. 8:27-The waters are round
Jer. 10:12-Einstein's theory, $E=MC^2$
Joel 2:5-Describes airplanes and jets
Ezek. 38:9 and Jer. 4:13-More about airplanes
Zech. 14:12-Effects of atomic radiation
Job 38:7-The stars "sing," have a vocal quality
Isa. 50:3-The heavens are black
Job 28:25-Air has weight
Job 25:5-The moon doesn't have its own light
Jer. 33:22-The stars cannot be numbered
Eccl. 1:6-The wind travels in circuits
Jer. 5:22-The ocean doesn't overflow
Job 28:5-The earth has fire inside
Jer. 6:22-The earth has sides (not flat like a plate)
Job 38:31-Earth rotates around the axle star
Lev. 17:11-Life of the flesh is in the blood

I Cor. 15:39-All flesh is not the same flesh (Parke Davis pharmaceutical house discovered the "antihuman precipitin" test which establishes the identity of different kinds of flesh- whether it be human, dog, cat, buzzard, etc.)

10. The Bible gives a detailed picture of the promised Messiah in the Old Testament, many of the prophecies given hundreds of years before His birth. Thirty-three of these were fulfilled in one day! (See Chapter 12 on "The Jew" for a partial list of these prophecies.)

"Suppose," says Dr. Olinthus Gregory, "that there were only 50 prophecies in the Old Testament (instead of 333) concerning the first advent of Christ, giving details of the coming Messiah and all meet in the person of Jesus... the probability of chance fulfillment as calculated by mathematicians according to the theory of probabilities is less than one in 1,125,000,000,000,000.

Now add only two more elements to these 50 prophecies, and fix the TIME and the PLACE at which they must happen and the immense improbability that they will take place by chance exceeds all the power of numbers to express..." (Messiah in Both Testaments, by Meldau, page eight).

11. The Dead Sea Scrolls-Some critics, desperately seeking some loopholes in prophecy (because they KNOW fulfilled prophecy is a DEFINITE PROOF that the Bible could not have been written by man, because of man's inability to constantly predict the future with a consistent degree of accuracy), used to say that books like Isaiah, Daniel, Micah, etc., were not really written before the New Testament but were merely recording history. Well, at least these infidels credit Christ with having FULFILLED the prophecies, anyway!

But the Dead Sea Scrolls, which are a collection of manuscripts found in the Dead Sea area, contain many of the writings of the ancient Essenes, and among them are found every book in the Old Testament except Esther, in whole or in part. Authorities agree (and it is now known throughout the literate world) that the books in the Old Testament were truly written long before the time of Christ, and thus they completely substantiate the prophecies as being 100% authentic. PRAISE THE LORD!

12. The Bible has stood the acid test of ENDURANCE! For nineteen centuries infidels have had their opportunities to demonstrate any error in the Word of God. The believers of the Bible have received constant ridicule and persecution, and yet the Bible still stands TRIED AND TRUE, and its message is still saving souls and giving strength and power to its followers.

CHAPTER XII—THE JEW

If you are well acquainted with many Jewish people you already know what intelligent, loving, and thoughtful people they are. If you have heard that Jews are "tight with money," you have learned that while they have sharp business acumen, they also are some of the most generous and tender-hearted people on the face of the earth when it comes to helping those in need.

The story of what the Jews went through in order to gain the statehood of Israel in May, 1948, is enough to break your heart, but it is the fulfillment of the Word of God that the Jews would be scattered, having no homeland for a long time, be persecuted, and after a long, hard struggle gain possession of the Land.

Because of the unusual and trying historical circumstances the Jewish nation has been through, if you, as a soulwinner, will adhere to the following suggestions as you witness to the Jewish people, you will perhaps be able to establish more rapport and be more effective in your presentation of their Messiah to them.

1. Somewhere in your conversation you might mention that if you were Jewish, you would be proud of it. A statement like this will help him realize you are not "anti-Semitic." It might evoke a question from him such as "Why would you be proud of being a Jew?" The Jews have been persecuted so much that sometimes they are a little suspicious of someone who says he loves the Jew... so you must be prepared to answer his question honestly and without hesitation. You might say that one reason you would be proud to be Jewish is that the Messiah was Jewish. Since God chose to take on Jewish flesh when He dwelt on earth, you would consider it an honor to be Jewish also. Another reason you would be proud to be Jewish can be expressed this way: "You see, nearly everything I know about God I've learned from the Jews, therefore, I owe them a great deal."

2. If you know they are Jewish, let them know you know it. Don't get nervous. This can be sensed right away. Just calmly present the gospel just as you would to anyone else, perhaps using more Old Testament verses than you ordinarily would.

3. It is usually beneficial to explain the difference between a Jew, a Gentile, and a Christian. Many people wrongly equate anyone who is a Gentile with Christian.

A Jew is a Jew from birth. It is his ancestry. A person who is Jewish can never stop being Jewish. If he later in life becomes a Catholic, a Baptist, or a Methodist, etc., this might affect his theological outlook, but he is still a Jew. His beliefs cannot change his physical birth.

A Gentile originally was anyone who was not a Jew. Thus, it would refer to any nationality other than Hebrew. Today, in a broader sense, it has come to refer to those who name the "Christian religion" as their own. However, we know from the Word of God that not every one who admires Jesus Christ really has accepted Him as Saviour, and this, perhaps, would be the case of many Gentiles.

A Christian is a Christian from birth... not from his physical birth into his physical family... but from his "second" birth (John 3:3; I Peter 1:23) into God's family (John 1:12, 13).

4. The good Christian loves the Jew. The true Christian knows the Messiah was a Jew and wants the Jews to accept their Messiah.

This does not mean that every Jewish person you meet will be a "lovely" person. Every Gentile is not a lovely person. No matter where you go, no matter what race of people you come across, you will always find those people you like and those people you do not like. But the dedicated Christian looks beyond an individual's personal characteristics, whether he be handsome and popular, or ugly and a social outcast, and sees instead a soul for whom Christ died, and who needs to have his sins forgiven by receiving Christ as his Saviour.

5. A good question to ask the Jewish person, as early in the conversation as you think would be wise, is: "Do you believe YOUR Bible?" Usually he will say "yes," and you will be able to use this later in the conversation as a reason why he should really put his faith in the Messiah... HIS Bible, the Old Testament, tells all about Him.

6. Be sure to mention that there is only one God and that you believe in only one God... the God of Abraham, Isaac, and Jacob.

An interesting passage is Deuteronomy 6: 4, "Hear, O Israel: The LORD our God is one Lord." In the Hebrew language and according to the Hebrew book of tradition, the Zoa, the words in this verse actually say that although God is one, God is also a trinity.

7. The Jewish person may fear that you are trying to "convert" him. Reassure him that if he accepts Christ as his Messiah, as his Saviour, he will still be a Jew, but a Jew who has his sins paid for.

8. All that we know about God and the Bible we owe to the Jews. Express your appreciation to them for the great part their nation had in giving us the Bible.

9. Abraham was a Gentile.

10. Israel is the chosen race. God chose Israel as the nation through which the Messiah would come.

11. Make it clear that the Jews were not the "Christ killers." Christ died voluntarily for all mankind. He gave His life for me. I am guilty in His death. Jesus said of His life, "No man taketh it from Me, but I lay it down of Myself. I have power to lay it down, and I have power to take it again. This commandment have I received of My Father" (John 10:18).

12. Praise the Old Testament prophets. Let them know you hold them in high esteem.

13. You might mention that all first Christians were Jewish. These early believers were surprised that Gentiles could be saved.

14. Percentage-wise there are more Jews who have accepted Christ as their Saviour than Gentiles. Most Jewish people do not realize this, and it is a good thing to point out.

15. David Ben-Gurion, the great Jewish statesman, said, "Surely, these are the days of the Messiah, and if you listen closely, you can hear His footsteps."

16. Point out that the Scriptures speak of TWO comings of the Messiah. The first would be one of suffering and death. "Of which salvation the prophets have inquired and searched diligently, who prophesied of the grace that should come unto you: Searching what, or what manner of time the Spirit of Christ which was in them did signify, when it testified beforehand the SUFFERINGS OF CHRIST, and the glory that should follow" (I Peter 1:10, 11).

Christ knew He would be rejected, "For as the lightning, that lighteneth out of the one part under heaven, shineth unto the other part under heaven: so shall also the Son of man be in His day. BUT FIRST must He suffer many things, and be rejected of this generation" (Luke 17:24, 25).

ORTHODOX JUDAISM

In some parts of the country there are very few Orthodox Jews. In these same areas Orthodox young people will also be extremely rare. Orthodox Judaism, though it has added a great deal of tradition to its beliefs, approaches the Bible more literally than other Jews. They have a long history of looking for the Messiah, and as far as they are concerned, He has not yet come. Centuries have passed, and they are still waiting. It's only natural for doubts and disappointments to creep in, and this disappointment often turns to discouragement. As a result, Conservative and Reformed Judaism (with their spiritualizing of Scripture) have come upon the scene.

My heart is really sorrowful for the Orthodox Jews who don't accept Christ as their Messiah. They believe the Old Testament is the Word of God, and they are trying to keep God's law as best they can-and yet they don't find favor in God's eyes because they reject God's Son.

The Apostle Paul said, "Brethren, my heart's desire and prayer to God for Israel is, that they might be saved. For I bear them record, that they have a zeal of God, but not according to knowledge. For they being ignorant of God's righteousness, and going about to establish their own righteousness, have not submitted themselves unto the righteousness of God. For Christ is the end of the law for righteousness to every one that believeth" (Romans 10:1-4).

A person can become so wrapped up in religious ceremony, tradition of his family, and the habit patterns formed during his childhood, that he continues in his religious observances without really considering the reasons (or considering if there BE reasons) behind these practices.

Jesus told the Pharisees (those very devout Jews) that this was their problem. "He answered and said unto them, Well hath Esaias prophesied of you hypocrites, as it is written, This people honoureth Me with their lips, but their heart is far from Me. Howbeit in vain do they worship Me, teaching for doctrines the commandments of men. For laying aside the commandment of God, ye hold the tradition of men... Full well ye reject the commandment of God, that ye may keep your own tradition" (Mark 7:6-9).

It is inconceivable to me that an Orthodox rabbi could be as unfamiliar with Messianic prophecy as some of them are. You would think it would be their main concern. Some Orthodox rabbis I have spoken to actually admitted they had never read the fifty-third chapter of Isaiah before! This lack of knowing the Scriptures is a terrible situation, because how can they teach the people in their Temple what they do not even know themselves? No wonder so many have left the Orthodox synagogue! The prophet Jeremiah commented on this: "For the pastors are become brutish, and have NOT SOUGHT THE LORD: therefore they shall not prosper, and all their flocks shall be scattered" (Jeremiah 10:21).

I wouldn't want to be in the position of leading a group of people if my leadership was contrary to the Word of God and caused the people to go astray. "WOE be unto the pastors that destroy and scatter the sheep of My pasture! saith the Lord" (Jeremiah 23:1).

The Orthodox Jews have been following their traditions for so long and remained true to their heritage at such a cost, that sometimes it is very difficult to lead them to the Lord even when they see the truths (academically) in the Bible.

Their emotions play a great part in their thinking about religion. Their love and respect for their parents and loving concern for their children enter considerably into their feelings of not wanting to "convert" from Judaism to Christianity.

If you are very careful, you can often take this love for their family and use it in such a way that they will WANT to trust Christ. For instance, take an Orthodox Jew who has already had a parent die. When he understands from the Bible that in order to go to heaven a person must believe in Jesus, he may refuse Christ as his Saviour simply because he doesn't want to go to heaven if his loved one isn't going to be there.

Here is how you can take this objection and turn it into the very reason he SHOULD trust Christ as his Saviour.... You might present it to him this way: If his loved one is in heaven, surely that loved one wants him to go to heaven also... but if that loved one is in hell, he or she CERTAINLY doesn't want him to go to hell. The loved one wouldn't be that selfish!

An example from Scripture of a man in hell and how he wants his family on earth to be witnessed to and warned of the torment is found in Luke 16:27, 28, "Then he said, I pray thee therefore, Father, that thou wouldest send him to my father's house: for I have five brethren; that he may testify unto them, lest they also come into this place of torment."

An approach like this has been successful in many cases. One thing that should definitely help you as you witness to the Orthodox Jew is that he claims to believe the Old Testament, and you can bear down heavily on Old Testament prophetic and salvation verses and lovingly and firmly insist that if he believes his Bible, he must believe what these verses are saying.

Conservative and Reformed Judaism

Conservative Judaism is very similar to many Protestant churches today in that it has slipped away from the Orthodox theological position while still trying to retain much of its tradition.

While claiming to consider the Old Testament as their guide, Conservative Jews do not necessarily accept the teaching therein as directly from God and do not take the Scriptures literally. Therefore, you have the same problem in witnessing to them as you would in witnessing to many Protestants in that they do not really believe what the Bible is saying. You will probably need to explain why we know the Bible is the Word of God.

Often the people who attend a Conservative synagogue do so more to keep up their family traditions than as an actual expression of any deep religious convictions. They are usually very uninformed about Judaism itself and are grossly ignorant of the Word of God.

The Reformed Jewish Synagogue is the most radical of the Jewish groups. Most Orthodox Jews wish the Reformed Jews wouldn't even use the word "Jew" since they deny the very basic fundamentals of Jewish theology.

The EXTENT of their departure from orthodoxy was brought home to me three years ago during an interview I had with the rabbi of a well-known Reformed Temple in Coral Gables. Below is an almost verbatim copy of our conversation... you may be shocked.

1. When asked if he believed in God, he said, "To put it bluntly, no!" He could offer no definition of God.

2. When asked what he thought would happen to him when he died, he said, "I do not know. I do not think it will make any difference."

3. In answer to my question, "Don't you CARE what happens to you when you die?" he replied, "No, not at all."

4. I said, "But this is so very important. Isn't it important to you to know the truth about God?" He said, "No. There are many important things I know nothing about. Why should I worry about it?"

5. He said he does not believe in heaven or hell, but that he thinks there is probably something after death, though he does not have any idea what it is.

6. He said he does not believe in anything "that is not experienced today. If it doesn't happen today, it is not true. Since people do not walk through an ocean today, no one walked through the Red Sea in times past."

7. He said, "My children learn about the myth of Achilles' heel in school. I do not expect them to believe it is true. They learn about the Bible, too, and I do not expect them to believe it is true either. While both stories have some truth somewhere, neither can be taken literally as truth."

8. He said, "The Bible says God created the heavens and earth in six days. This is absurd. It cannot be done in six days!" I asked, "Don't you believe God can do anything He wants to?" He replied, "I do not believe in God. I believe in evolution."

9. When I asked him, "Do you believe God has made any direct statements to people, so we could know Him?" he said, "I do not believe God ever 'said' anything to any one."

10. I asked, "Don't you believe Moses received his writings from God?" He answered, "I do not believe any of the characters in the Bible wrote what 'God said.'" "When they claimed inspiration," I asked, "do you think they were lying?" "Yes," he replied, "they were deceived by their own ideas. Many books claim they wrote a message straight from God, and I do not believe any of them, including the Bible."

11. When I asked him why he didn't believe the Bible, he said, "It is full of contradictions, scientific and medical errors, and historical inaccuracies. The Bible just does not measure up to today's knowledge." When I asked him to show me just ONE of any of these errors, he said, "I do not have time. It would involve too much technical study."

12. He suggested that if I went to "college or even a 'Christian' seminary," I would not believe the Bible when I got out. He said even Christian ministers today don't believe the Bible! (This certainly is a sad commentary coming from a Jewish rabbi.)

13. When I brought up the subject of the Messiah, he said, "None of the Old Testament people looked for any 'Messiah.' You are reading into the Scriptures. Only recently has anyone looked for a 'Messiah'."

14. I said I would be glad to buy any book he would recommend that would support his position of the Bible being inaccurate, etc. He said, "I do not care to recommend any. ASK YOUR MINISTER FOR ONE. If your beliefs leave you comfortable, you are O.K." I pressed him to show me any error of any kind in the Bible and he just would not (or could not).

15. When I offered to leave him some literature, free of charge, proving the Bible is the Word of God, he said, "I don't want it, and I won't read it." He said our conversation was unfruitful because I had a mental block of wanting to believe the Bible, and he did not want to talk any further with such a bigoted person!

Messianic Prophecy

Isaiah 7:14, "Therefore the Lord Himself shall give you a sign; Behold, a virgin shall conceive, and bear a son, and shall call His Name Immanuel."

Jewish people say they will expect a "sign" from God when the Messiah comes, so they will know that He is truly the Messiah. God has already given them their "sign" at the birth of Jesus. Mary was a virgin and yet had conceived. This was the sign God promised. Mary was the mother of the flesh God took upon Himself when He came to earth. Jesus had no earthly father because the Holy Spirit gave Mary conception, not a man.

Notice the fulfillment in Matthew 1:20-25, "But while he (Joseph) thought on these things, behold, the angel of the Lord appeared unto him in a dream, saying, Joseph, thou son of David, fear not to take unto thee Mary thy wife: for that which is conceived in her is OF THE HOLY GHOST.

"And she shall bring forth a son, and thou shalt call His Name JESUS: for He shall save His people from their sins.

"Now all this was done, that it might be fulfilled which was spoken of THE LORD by the prophet, saying, "Behold, a VIRGIN shall be with child, and shall bring forth a son, and they shall call His Name Emmanuel, which being interpreted is, GOD WITH US.

"Then Joseph being raised from sleep did as the angel of the Lord had bidden him, and took unto him his wife:

"And KNEW HER NOT TILL she had brought forth her firstborn son: and he called His Name JESUS."

Isaiah 9:6, "For unto us a child is born, unto us a son is given: and the government shall be upon His shoulder: and His Name shall be called Wonderful, Counsellor, The mighty God, The everlasting Father, The Prince of Peace."

Notice, the Son of God wasn't born-the Son of God always has been. But "God so loved the world, that He gave His only begotten Son...." The flesh the Son of God took upon Himself was born. And who is this Son of God? He is the mighty God. He is the everlasting Father. Jesus was not "another" God. Jesus is God Himself who came to earth in the form of a human being so He could pay for our sins.

At the birth of Christ, Luke records, "Blessed be the Lord God of Israel; for He (the Lord God) hath visited and redeemed His people." "And the angel of the Lord said unto them, Fear not: for, behold, I bring you good tidings of great joy, which shall be to all people. For unto you is born this day in the city of David a Saviour, which is Christ, the Lord" (Luke 1:68; 2:10, 11).

Micah 5:2, "But thou, Bethlehem Ephratah, though thou be little among the thousands of Judah, yet out of thee shall He come forth unto me that is to be ruler in Israel; whose goings forth have been from of old, from everlasting."

There were two Bethlehems at that time, one being Bethlehem Ephratah and the other Bethlehem Zebulon. Notice that God is specific in His prophecies. Who was this that would come out of Bethlehem Ephratah? Someone who has been alive forever previously, "from everlasting." This is a characteristic belonging only to God.

Isaiah Chapter Fifty-Three

v. 1, "Who hath believed our report? and to whom is the arm of the LORD revealed?" This is a prophecy that the nation Israel, as a whole, would reject the Messiah. Its fulfillment is recorded in John 12:37, 38, "But though He had done so many miracles before them, yet they believed not on Him: That the saying of Esaias the prophet might be fulfilled, when he spake, Lord, who hath believed our report? and to whom hath the arm of the Lord been revealed?"

v. 2, "For He shall grow up before him as a tender plant, and as a root out of a dry ground: He hath no form nor comeliness; and when we shall see Him, there is no beauty that we should desire Him." Contrary to some artists' conceptions of the beauty of Jesus, according to this verse He was not handsome. It is better that people should love Him for WHO He is, than for appearance.

v. 3, "He is despised and rejected of men; a man of sorrows, and acquainted with grief: and we hid as it were our faces from Him; He was despised; and we esteemed Him not." Jesus was despised then, and He is despised now. How heartbreaking it must be! "He was in the world, and the world was made by Him, and the world knew Him not. He came unto His own, and His own received Him not" (John 1:10, 11). God came to earth IN PERSON, and the world didn't recognize Him. What an oversight!

v. 4, "Surely He hath borne our griefs, and carried our sorrows: yet we did esteem Him stricken, smitten of God, and afflicted." Jesus understands all the sorrow and trouble the Jewish nation has gone through, and He loves them with an everlasting love and wants them to find rest in Him. "O Jerusalem, Jerusalem, thou that killest the prophets, and stonest them which are sent unto thee, how often would I have gathered thy children together, even as a hen gathereth her chickens under her wings, and YE would not!" (Matt. 23:37) Instead of the Jews realizing their Messiah had come, they thought the crucifixion was God's judgment upon a false prophet, a blasphemer (John 10:33).

v. 5, "But He was wounded for OUR transgressions, He was bruised for OUR iniquities: the chastisement of OUR peace was upon Him; and with His stripes WE are healed." Notice that four times in this one verse alone, the substitutionary death of Christ is referred to.

The New Testament says, "Who His own self bare OUR sins in His own body on the tree, that WE being dead to sins, should live unto righteousness: by whose stripes YE were healed" (I Peter 2:24).

WE are guilty. WE are sinners. Christ was not. WE deserve to pay for our sins. Christ didn't deserve that cruel death on the cross. But because He loves us, He paid the price of our sins.

v. 6, "All we like sheep have gone astray; we have turned every one to his own way; and the Lord hath laid on HIM the iniquity of us all." THIS IS THE MAIN SALVATION VERSE YOU WILL PROBABLY USE IN LEADING A JEWISH PERSON TO THE LORD. (The hand gesture, illustrated in Chapter 23, was used with this verse by R. A. Torrey. He mentions this in his book, Personal Work.) We recommend that you practice this hand gesture and USE IT... especially with verses like Isaiah 53:6.

The New Testament complement to Isaiah 53:6 is II Cor. 5:21. "For He hath made Him to be sin for us, who knew no sin; that we might be made the righteousness of God in Him." The hand gesture is also effectively used with this verse, demonstrating the fact that WE are the sinners, but CHRIST made the payment for our sin. The Jewish person today has no payment for his sin. The sacrifices described in the Old Testament as a covering for sin until the Messiah would come were halted by the destruction of Herod's Temple in 70 A.D. by Titus. (The REAL reason, of course, that there are no more sacrifices is that Christ made the SACRIFICE OF HIMSELF, once and for all, to be the sacrifice God would accept for all sin, for all people, for all time. See the 9th and 10th chapters of Hebrews.)

Hosea 3:4 prophesies of the time when the Jews would no longer have a sacrifice. "For the children of Israel shall abide many days without a king (they have none), and without a prince (they have none), and without a sacrifice (they have none)."

v. 8, "He was taken from prison and from judgment: and who shall declare His generation? For He was CUT OFF out of the land of the living: for the transgression of my people was He stricken." Many Jewish people do not realize there were to be TWO comings of the Messiah. Verses like this will show them that at Christ's first coming He was to be CUT OFF (rather than to set up the Davidic Kingdom). The first coming of Christ was humble. The second coming shall be glorious! (Matt. 24:30)

v. 10, "Yet it pleased the LORD to bruise Him; He hath put Him to grief: when thou shalt make His soul an OFFERING FOR SIN, He shall see His seed, He shall prolong His days, and the pleasure of the Lord shall prosper in His hand." Jesus would die-His soul would be an OFFERING FOR SIN, and yet His days would be prolonged.... He would come back from the dead!

v. 11, "He shall see of the travail of His soul, and shall be satisfied: by His knowledge shall my righteous servant justify many; for He shall BEAR THEIR INIQUITIES." God will be satisfied with the payment Christ will make for sin. Today we know He was satisfied, because if sin had not been fully paid for, Christ could not have come back from the dead (Rom. 6:23; 4:25). Christ bore our iniquities and many have been made righteous by receiving this payment He made for them.

Daniel 9:26, "And after threescore and two weeks shall Messiah be CUT OFF, but not for Himself: and the people of the prince that shall come shall destroy the city (Jerusalem) and the sanctuary (the Temple); and the end thereof shall be with a flood and unto the end of the war desolations are determined."

This is one of the strongest verses proving that the Messiah God spoke about has already been here... because this verse says the Messiah will be CUT OFF, and that AFTER HE is cut off, Jerusalem and the Temple will be destroyed. It is common knowledge that Titus, in 70 A.D., had Jerusalem and the Temple destroyed, and today the Mosque of Omar stands where the Temple once stood.

Zechariah 12:10, "And I will pour upon the house of David, and upon the inhabitants of Jerusalem, the spirit of grace and of supplications: and they shall look upon ME WHOM THEY HAVE PIERCED, and they shall mourn for Him, as one mourneth for his only son...."

This whole chapter is "The burden of the Word of the LORD for Israel, saith the LORD..." (v. 1), and the Lord is speaking throughout. God is saying that in the latter times people will look upon HIM whom they have pierced. This can only be referring to God the Son at the crucifixion.

Proverbs 30:4, "Who hath ascended up into heaven or descended? Who hath gathered the wind in His fists? Who hath bound the waters in a garment? Who hath established all the ends of the earth? What is His Name, and what is His SON'S Name, if thou canst tell?"

God has a Son! His Name is Immanuel, which, as we have seen, means "God dwelling with us." His Name is Jesus, which means "God who saves, and keeps," etc. Psalm 2:7, 8 also speak of God's Son. And yet this Son is the everlasting Father!

Presenting the Gospel

Throughout your witnessing bear in mind the suggestions given at the beginning of this chapter, inserting comments here and there as you witness that are appropriate in the conversation.

After you have established rapport, a good starting place is the Old Testament prophecies of the Messiah. (Using the term the "Messiah" instead of always saying "Christ" might be more easily taken by the Jewish person, although you need not shy away from saying "Christ" or "Jesus" when you want to.)

Below is a sample conversation with a Jewish person. If the things you are saying are well received, you can proceed right along. When there are questions or objections you will need to stop and answer them, being careful not to get off too far from the gospel, so you can easily get back into it again.

Before going into the Messianic prophecy, briefly summarize the plan of salvation, and then go over the Scriptures.

WITNESS: "God loves you so much that He came to earth to make a complete payment for your sins so you could go to heaven and live with Him forever.

"I would like you to see some verses in your Bible, the Old Testament, that tell us how to recognize the true Messiah. God gave many specific requirements the Messiah would have to fulfill, and it is because Jesus has met these specifications that I know the Messiah has already come. Some of these are..." (Turn to them and let him read them.)

1. The Messiah had to be born of a virgin (Isa. 7:14). (The amount of detail you go into on each verse will depend upon the leading of the Holy Spirit in each case.)
2. Messiah had to be born in Bethlehem (Micah 5:2).
3. Messiah would be God Himself (Isa. 9:6).
4. Messiah would pay for sin (Isa. 53:6). (Use the hand gesture and explain the plan of salvation clearly.)
5. Messiah would come back from the dead (Isa. 53:10).
6. Jerusalem and the Temple would be destroyed AFTER the Messiah had come and given His life (Dan. 9:26).
7. The Messiah gave His life as a sacrifice for your sins. You need a blood sacrifice, and you have none now (Lev. 17:11).

"Since Jesus has met all the requirements of the Messiah, and since the Temple was destroyed in 70 A.D., doesn't it make sense to you that Jesus really was the Messiah?

"Wouldn't you like to accept Jesus as your Messiah, believing He made the payment for your sins on the cross, so you could go to heaven when you die? Remember, you will still be a Jew, but a Jew who has his sins paid for."

If you lovingly present the Messiah and His salvation to Jewish people, you will find many who will respond and accept Christ as their Saviour.

There are SO MANY Scriptures you can use with a Jewish person. It is best to use the more basic ones presented above. They will usually be sufficient.

Additional Prophecies About Christ and Their Fulfillments

1. Sold for 30 pieces of silver. Zech. 11:12; Matt. 26:15
2. Betrayed by a friend. Psalm 41:9; John 13:18
3. Silent before His accusers. Isa. 53:7; Mark 15:3-5
4. Hands and feet pierced. Psalm 22:16; the crucifixion
5. Garments divided by gambling. Psalm 22: 18; John 19: 24
6. Mocked. Psalm 22:7; Matt. 27:41
7. Gall and vinegar to drink. Psalm 69:21; Matt. 27:34
8. Prayed for His murderers. Isa. 53:12; Luke 23:34
9. Not a bone broken. Psalm 34:20; John 19:36
10. Crucified with thieves. Isa. 53:12; Mark 15:27, 28
11. His forsaken cry. Psalm 22: 1; Mark 15:34 12. His side pierced. Zech. 12:10; John 19:34-37
13. Buried with rich man. Isa. 53:9; Matt. 27:57-60
14. Looked on Him whom they pierced. Zech. 12: 10; John19:37
15. People esteemed and received Him not. Isa. 53:3; John 1:11

A question frequently asked by Jew and Gentile alike is: "How were people saved BEFORE Christ came and paid for sin?"

People living before Christ were saved when they by faith looked forward to the coming Messiah, believing He would come and pay for their sin-just like we today by faith look back to the time of Christ, believing He was the true Messiah and that He has paid for our sin.

For 1500 years the Jews had a distinct advantage over the Gentiles because God gave the Scriptures to the Jewish nation.

Romans 3: 1, 2 says, "What advantage then hath the Jew? Or what profit is there of circumcision? Much every way: chiefly because that UNTO THEM WERE COMMITTED THE ORACLES OF GOD."

However, many Jews have not taken advantage of their advantage! Having the Scriptures doesn't do them any good if they do not BELIEVE them.

Why has God blessed Gentiles and allowed them to be saved? Some Gentiles have received salvation while many Jews have not received it because of those Jews not seeking salvation BY FAITH.

Romans 9: 30-32, "What shall we say then? That the Gentiles, which followed not after righteousness, have attained to righteousness, even the righteousness which is OF FAITH. But Israel, which followed after the law of righteousness, hath not attained to the law of righteousness. WHEREFORE? Because they SOUGHT IT NOT BY FAITH, but as it were by the works of the law, for they stumbled at that stumblingstone."

Salvation is by faith now. Salvation has always been by faith. Salvation always will be by faith. Look up and study these references showing that salvation by faith was known to the Old Testament people.

Galatians 3:8
Habakkuk 2:4
I Corinthians 10: 1-4
Romans 4:6 II
Timothy 3: 15
Acts 15:11
John 8:56
Romans 3:21
Hebrews 4:2
Romans 1: 1, 2
I Corinthians 15:3, 4
Acts 3:18
Hebrews, chapter eleven

The Apostle Paul said, "For though I be free from all men, yet have I made myself servant unto all, that I might gain the more. And unto the Jews I became as a Jew, that I might gain the Jews... I am made all things to all men, that I might by all means save some. And this I do for the gospel's sake" (I Cor. 9:19, 20, 22, 23).

CHAPTER XIII—THE ROMAN CATHOLIC

YOUR COMMON GROUND

As believers there are some doctrines we do have in common (at least in part) with the Roman Catholic. However, Roman Catholic doctrines vary from decade to decade and from country to country.

Below are some doctrines you can use to establish some rapport with the Roman Catholic:

1. The Bible is God's Word. (Although they interpret it by the dictates of the Pope and their tradition.)
2. Jesus is God. (Although they elevate the Pope and Mary to heights of glory belonging only to Christ.)
3. Man needs a Saviour. (Although they don't believe Jesus alone can save man through man's faith in His payment for all their sin on the cross.)
4. There is a heaven and a hell. (Although they also believe in limbo and purgatory, which are not taught in the Scriptures... and they do not teach the difference between going to heaven or hell is FAITH.)

GRACE AND WORKS

The main issue, the constant issue in witnessing to Roman Catholics, is grace and works. The Church has set up myriads of rites, rituals, and rules which its subjects (and I use the word advisedly) must follow if they are to have any hopes of reaching heaven someday (maybe even centuries after they die).

It is amazing but true that when a group is "off" on grace and works, almost every other doctrine it holds is also affected by the poison. As God said in Galatians 5:9, "A little leaven leaveneth the whole lump."

There might be a time when you are witnessing to a Roman Catholic and think you have just gotten the plan of salvation really ACROSS to the person. But then he will make a comment or ask a question that will tell you right away that he really doesn't understand salvation is by faith and not of works.

The reason he doesn't understand the gospel is because teaching after teaching has been drilled into his head ever since he was a tiny child that salvation is not by faith alone, and that many more things than just faith are required of the person wanting to go to heaven.

From every side the error is brought in, and sometimes the reasons behind the doctrines are subtle-subtle with the cunning and wickedness of Satan. And again we warn you, as Paul warned those in his care, "But I fear, lest by any means, as the serpent beguiled Eve through his subtilty, so your minds should be corrupted from the simplicity that is in Christ." And, "Beware lest any man spoil you through philosophy and vain deceit, after the tradition of men, after the rudiments of the world, and NOT AFTER CHRIST" (II Cor. 11:3; Col. 2:8).

The Catholics' loud claims that the Church was built upon Peter ... the adoration of saints... the exaltation of Mary... if Christ had brothers... confession to the priest... the rosary... YOU COULD ARGUE ALL DAY AND NIGHT WITH A CATHOLIC ABOUT THESE THINGS AND YET NEVER LEAD HIM TO KNOW CHRIST AS HIS SAVIOUR!

If you have been born again, you have the Holy Spirit indwelling you and enlightening your mind with a clear understanding of Scripture on all these things... but the person who has been brought up in the Catholic Church is probably NOT born again, and so does NOT have the benefit of the Holy Spirit teaching him DETAILS in the Word of God (even if they are important details).

What is the Holy Spirit busy convincing the world of? John 16:8-11 teaches us the Holy Spirit is convincing the world of sin, that they lack righteousness, and that judgment is coming. And why are they being convinced of sin? Because they do not BELIEVE on Christ as their Saviour (16:9).

If you want to do your witnessing in COOPERATION with what the Holy Spirit is trying to do in the lives of unbelievers... speak about the GOSPEL... how the person can be saved... that salvation is a gift of God received by faith... and leave the OTHER QUESTIONS to be answered (as much as possible) AFTER the person is saved!

Jesus Paid for all Sin

In the Roman Catholic doctrine, sin is compartmentalized. There is venial sin which the Baltimore Catechism No. 3 defines this way: "What is venial sin? Venial sin is a less serious offense against the law of God, which does not deprive the soul of sanctifying grace, and which can be pardoned even without sacramental confession."

There is also, in the Catholic doctrine, mortal sin. "What is mortal sin? Mortal sin is a grievous offense against the law of God. Why is this sin called mortal? This sin is called mortal, or deadly, because it deprives the sinner of sanctifying grace, the supernatural life of the soul. Besides depriving the sinner of sanctifying grace, what else does mortal sin do to the soul? Besides depriving the sinner of sanctifying grace, mortal sin makes the soul an enemy of God, takes away the merit of all of its good actions, deprives it of the right to everlasting happiness in heaven, and makes it deserving of everlasting punishment in hell."

The Catholic Church also recognizes Adamic sin, that is, the sin or sin nature which man inherits from Adam. It is for the Adamic sin that Christ supposedly died. You must show the Catholic that Jesus Christ has completely paid the full price for all of his sin.

First, show from Scripture that all sin is mortal, or deadly (James 2:10; Rom. 6:23). Second, use Scripture to show that all sin- no matter how one classifies it-has been paid for by Christ (Heb. 1:3; I Pet. 2:24; 3:18; I John 2:2).

"Be it known unto you therefore, men and brethren, that through this Man is preached unto you the forgiveness of sins: And by Him all that believe are justified from ALL things, from which ye could not be justified by the law of Moses" (Acts 13:38, 39).

Even keeping the commandments would not "justify you from all things." In the first place, no one has kept them. In the second place, keeping the commandments still wouldn't make you perfect. Hebrews 7:19 says, "For the law made NOTHING perfect, but the bringing in of a better hope did (Jesus, v. 22); by the which we draw nigh unto God."

JESUS is the only way to heaven. "Jesus saith unto him, I am THE way, THE truth, and THE life: no man cometh unto the Father but by Me." Salvation is not in a church. It is not in the Mormon church. It is not in the Protestant church. It is not in the Roman Catholic church. Salvation is in a Person. Salvation is in Jesus. "For the law was given by Moses, but grace and truth came by Jesus Christ" (John 1: 17).

How Can We be Cleansed of Sin?

When a Roman Catholic sins, he is supposed to do several things:

(1) Go to the priest and confess his sin.

(2) Receive from the priest the penance he is to do, and go home and do it. (This often consists of reciting a certain number of "rosaries," "Lord's Prayers," etc.)
(3) Go to Mass.
(4) Be arranging for people to pray for his soul after he dies, so his soul can be released from purgatory in time.

To a person who has received the Lord Jesus Christ as his Saviour, God says of his sins: "And you, being dead in your sins and the uncircumcision of your flesh, hath He quickened together with Him, having forgiven you ALL TRESPASSES; blotting out the handwriting of ordinances that was against us, which was contrary to us, and took it out of the way, nailing it to His cross" (Col. 2:13, 14).

The Christian does not need another offering (Mass) for his sins. "For by ONE offering, He (Christ) hath perfected FOREVER them that are sanctified (made pure and holy)" (Heb. 10:14). "Now where remission of these is, there is NO MORE OFFERING FOR SIN" (Heb. 10:18).

The Roman Catholic is forever trying to re-crucify Christ... all in vain. Christ's ONE death on the cross paid for ALL sin of ALL people for ALL time for EVERYONE who would receive that payment by faith.

When the Priest Offers the Sacrifice of Mass

"And every priest standeth daily ministering and offering oftentimes the same sacrifices which can NEVER take away sins" (Heb. 10:11).

Whatever the Catholic might think the sacrifice of Mass can do for him, ONE THING we know it can NOT do. IT CAN NOT TAKE AWAY SINS!

It is God's will that the sacrifice of Christ would pay for all sin, and that those who would receive that payment would be made pure and holy in God's eyes forever. "By the which will we are sanctified through the offering of the body of Jesus Christ once for all" (Heb. 10:10).

The Catholic Church teaches that Mass is the sacrifice of Christ OVER AGAIN for sins. But Romans 6:9 says, "KNOWING that Christ being raised from the dead DIETH NO MORE...."

The problem with the Catholic is that he doesn't really believe Christ paid for ALL his sin. And yet the Bible is very clear, "Who gave Himself for us, that He might redeem us from ALL iniquity..." (Titus 2:14).

This is why it is a problem of grace and works. God says salvation is by grace. The Catholic will not deny this. But at the same time he believes he must follow rituals and rules to make this grace of God effective on his behalf. And this is unscriptural. What verse shows that if salvation is of grace, then it cannot be of works as well? I hope you said, "Romans 11:6."

Do you see that what the Catholic needs most, then, is for you to go over the plan of salvation with him, simply and with Scripture, showing him that THE BIBLE says salvation is "by grace through faith"? It might take a long time for the "light to break through." But be patient. Remember, his parents, his teachers, his priest, even the Pope, have been teaching him contrary to the Word of God on this subject of salvation all of his life.

It is only when the Catholic seems REALLY bothered by some other question that you should spend any length of time on anything other than salvation itself, or after he is saved.

But for your own information, the following are some errors in the Roman Catholic theology and the correct teachings from Scripture.

1. The Roman Catholic worships Christ, but worships Him in vain. "But in vain they do worship Me, teaching for doctrines the commandments of men" (Matt. 15:9). See also Galatians 5:1-4.

2. They teach that Peter was the first Pope and that the Popes are to exercise authority over the people. However, this is contrary to what Peter himself expressed in Scripture. "The elders which are among you I exhort, who am also AN ELDER (not one Pope, but one among many elders), and a witness of the sufferings of Christ, and also a partaker of the glory that shall be

revealed: FEED the flock of God which is among you, taking the oversight thereof, NOT BY CONSTRAINT, but willingly; NOT FOR FILTHY LUCRE, but of a ready mind; NEITHER AS BEING LORDS over God's heritage, but being ensamples to the flock" (I Peter 5: 1-3).

The Bible never teaches that the spiritual leader of the flock is to be the "boss." The leader is to give positive leadership, yes, but not to try to play "God" in people's lives.

Scripture is full of evidence that the true spiritual leader will be a SERVANT of the people rather than some boss.

"For we preach not ourselves, but Christ Jesus the Lord; and ourselves YOUR SERVANTS for Jesus' sake" (II Cor. 4:5).

Jesus had much to say along this line. "But Jesus called them to Him, and saith unto them, Ye know that they which are accounted to rule over the Gentiles exercise lordship over them; and their great ones exercise authority upon them.

"But so shall it NOT be among you: but whosoever will be great among you, shall be your MINISTER. And whosoever of you will be the chiefest, shall be SERVANT of all.

"For even the Son of man came not to be ministered unto, but to minister, and to give His life a ransom for many" (Mark 10:42-45).

If you study much of the history of the Roman Catholic Church and the Papacy, you will see the magnitude of their error in exercising "lordship" over the flock.

3. Matthew 23: 9 says, "And call no man your father upon the earth: for one is your Father, which is in heaven." The Catholics make a great mistake in that they demand reverence of human beings. Only God should be worshipped. Other worship constitutes idolatry.

4. Veneration of Mary and the "Saints." Scripture says of Mary, "Hail, thou that art highly favoured, the Lord is with thee: blessed art thou among women" (Luke 1:28). Mary was a wonderful, godly woman. But Mary, like everyone, was still a sinner (Rom. 3:23). She herself acknowledged God as her SAVIOUR, "And Mary said, My soul doth magnify the Lord. And my spirit hath rejoiced in God my Saviour" (Luke 1:46, 47). A person who isn't a sinner doesn't need salvation, and thus doesn't have a Saviour.

Scripture teaches that all believers are saints. The word has the meaning of "pure and holy ones." All those who have received the Lord Jesus Christ as their Saviour are "pure and holy" through the righteousness God gives to them (I Cor. 1:30; II Cor. 5:21; etc.). The Apostles referred to the whole group of Christians as "saints" (Eph. 1:1; II Cor. 1:1; Phil. 1:1; etc.), and not just to those in a select group. God makes a person a saint; man does not. God points out the person as a saint; man does not. God sets us the conditions of being a saint; man does not... and neither does the Roman Catholic Church.

5. The Pope, the priest, Mary, the saints... none of these can mediate between God and man. "For there is one God, and ONE MEDIATOR between God and men, the man CHRIST JESUS" (I Tim. 2:5). The believer is invited to come straight to the Lord, through Jesus, in time of need.

"Seeing then that we have a great high priest, that is passed into the heavens, Jesus the Son of God, let us hold fast our profession. For we have not an high priest which can not be touched with the feeling of our infirmities; but was in all points tempted like as we are, yet without sin. Let us therefore come BOLDLY UNTO THE THRONE OF GRACE, that we may obtain mercy, and find grace to help in time of need" (Heb. 4:14-16).

"Having therefore, brethren, boldness to enter into the holiest BY THE BLOOD OF JESUS, by a new and living way, which He hath consecrated for us, through the veil, that is to say, His flesh" (Heb. 10:19, 20).

"Therefore being justified by faith, we have peace with God through our Lord Jesus Christ: by whom also we have access by faith into this grace wherein we stand..." (Rom. 5:1, 2).

6. Whom should we confess our sins to? The Catholic Church says we should confess them to the priest. The Bible says only God can forgive sins, and that we should confess our sins to Jesus, because He is our advocate-He is our intercessor.

"If we confess our sins, He is faithful and just to forgive us our sins, and to cleanse us from all unrighteousness... and if any man sin, we have an advocate with the Father, Jesus Christ the righteous" (I John 1:9; 2:1). Our advocate is not Mary, nor the priest... our advocate is Jesus!

7. Purgatory is not mentioned in the Bible. There is no "place of cleansing" other than the blood of Jesus Christ. I John 1:7 says "... the BLOOD OF JESUS CHRIST His Son cleanseth us from all sin."

One of the things that caused Martin Luther to speak up against the Roman Catholic Church and its practices regarding the sale of indulgences was remarks made like, "The moment you hear your money drop in the box, the soul of your mother will jump out of purgatory," by Tetzel, a Dominican Friar (The Church in History, by B. K. Kuiper, page 160). Indulgences were sold to people who went to the priest for penance, and who would rather pay a sum of money to the Church than do some other form of penalty or satisfaction for their sin. In time, indulgences were also sold to those who were trying to help the soul of a departed one to go from purgatory to heaven. The people found it easier to pay a sum of money for the soul of a dear one than to spend all the time otherwise required for them to pray for them. This system pleased the Church very much, as it gave them an amazingly large source of revenue. It is said that the St. Peter's Cathedral in Rome was built through the sale of these indulgences.

This whole concept is so out of keeping with Scripture! "Forasmuch as ye KNOW that ye were not redeemed with corruptible things, as silver and gold, from your vain conversation received by tradition from your fathers; but with the PRECIOUS BLOOD of Christ, as of a lamb without blemish and without spot" (I Peter 1:18, 19).

"But Peter said unto him, Thy money perish with thee, because thou has thought that the GIFT OF GOD may be purchased with money" (Acts 8:20).

It is not within the power of human beings to in any way aid in the redemption of another person. (You cannot even redeem your own soul, for that matter.)

"None of them can by ANY MEANS redeem his brother, nor give to God a ransom for him" (Psalm 49:7).

"The soul that sinneth, it shall die. The son shall not bear the iniquity of the father, neither shall the father bear the iniquity of the son..." (Ezekiel 18:20).

The Bible teaches that if a person is lost, he goes to hell. If a person is saved, he goes to be with the Lord in heaven. There is no such thing as purgatory. "... to depart, and to be with Christ..." (Phil. 1:23). "We are confident, I say, and willing rather to be absent from the body, and to be PRESENT WITH THE LORD" (II Cor. 5:8). "For we know that if our earthly house of this tabernacle were dissolved, we have a building of God, an house not made with hands, eternal in the HEAVENS" (II Cor. 5:1).

Once a person has received Christ as his Saviour, he does not have to worry about being condemned for his sin. Punished on earth, and without much reward in heaven, yes... but condemned to purgatory for a time, or to hell for eternity... NO!

"Verily, verily, I say unto you, He that heareth My word, and believeth on Him that sent Me, HATH EVERLASTING LIFE, and shall NOT come into condemnation: but is PASSED from death unto life" (John 5:24).

If there were such a place as purgatory, Jesus certainly left it out of His remarks. Jesus said to the thief on the cross, "Today shalt thou be with Me in paradise." If the thief went to purgatory, then Jesus was a liar.

8. The Catholics say Mary remained a virgin all her life, and that Christ had no flesh and blood sisters or brothers. (He did have half-brothers and sisters, as Joseph was not the father of Christ.) "Is not this the carpenter, the son of Mary, the BROTHER of James, and Joses, and of Juda, and Simon? And are not his SISTERS here with us?" (Mark 6:3)

9. "Forbidding to marry and commanding to abstain from meats." Is this doctrine of the Catholic Church from the Bible... from the Lord?

"Now the Spirit speaketh expressly, that in the latter times some shall depart from the faith, giving heed to seducing spirits, and doctrines of DEVILS, SPEAKING LIES in hypocrisy; having their conscience seared with a hot iron: forbidding to marry, and commanding to abstain from meats, which God hath created to be RECEIVED with thanksgiving of them which believe and know the truth" (I Tim. 4:1-3).

"Let no man therefore judge you in meat, or in drink, or in respect of an holyday, or of the new moon, or of the sabbath days" (Col. 2:16). "Let no man beguile (defraud) you of your reward in a voluntary humility and worshiping of angels, intruding into those things which he hath not seen, vainly puffed up by his fleshly mind... Wherefore if ye be dead with Christ from the rudiments of the world, WHY, as though living in the world, are ye subject to ordinances, (Touch not; taste not; handle not; which all are to perish with the using;) after the commandments and doctrines of men? Which things have indeed a shew of wisdom in will worship and humility, and neglecting of the body; not in any honour to the satisfying of the flesh" (Col. 2: 18, 20-23).

The Scofield Reference Bible makes the notation in regard to this verse, "Which do not really honour God, but only satisfy the flesh (i.e., by creating a reputation for superior sanctity)."

The Catholic system of self-imposed worship and self humiliation and degradation, thinking that somehow this would please God, is actually contrary to Scripture, as human logic often is.

Christ said in Matt. 9:13, "... I will have MERCY, and NOT SACRIFICE: for I am not come to call the righteous, but sinners to repentance (to change their minds)."

It is the sacrifice of Christ that God looks at for our salvation, not any sacrifice we might make for Him. However, after we are saved, we are invited to serve the Lord-but this is our REASONABLE service, rather than a sacrifice. It is to our benefit, both now and later.

10. The Catholic Church teaches that the "true church" (their church) is built upon Peter, using Matthew 16:18 as its textual basis for this claim.

Upon examination of this passage in Matthew 16, however, we do not find this teaching at all. Verses 13-16 record Jesus asking His disciples, "Whom do men say that I the Son of man am?" Simon Peter gives the correct answer, "Thou art the Christ, the Son of the living God." Peter knew Christ was God... the Son of God.

In verse 17 Jesus said, "Blessed art thou, Simon Barjona (son of Jonas): for flesh and blood hath not revealed it unto thee, but My Father which is in heaven." Jesus is saying that while He is the Son of God, Peter is the son of man.

Verse 18, "And I say also unto thee, That thou art Peter (petros), and upon this Rock (Petra) I will build My church; and the gates of hell shall not prevail against it." Jesus is saying, "Peter, you are a little stone, a small pebble. Upon this big Rock, this boulder (Christ) I will build My church."

I Cor. 3:11, "For other foundation can no man lay than that is laid, which is JESUS CHRIST"-not Peter. Jesus is the foundation upon which the true church is built.

Eph. 2: 20, "And are built upon the foundation of the apostles and prophets, JESUS CHRIST HIMSELF being the CHIEF CORNER STONE."

Even Peter himself speaks of believers as "stones," but of Christ as the "CHIEF CORNER STONE" (I Pet. 2: 4-8). Also see Acts 4:11.

11. The Catholic Church teaches water baptism is necessary for salvation. Please refer to Chapter Nine which covers this thoroughly.

The above eleven points, as we mentioned before, should rarely, if at all, be brought up during your presentation of the gospel to a Roman Catholic. If you do feel it is imperative to go into something along those lines for some reason, please do so with genuine love and patience. Remember, the person you are witnessing to did not make up these doctrines. Usually he believes them simply because this is what he has been taught, and he has not searched the Scriptures for himself, "whether those things were so."

If you really want to win Catholics (or anybody, for that matter) to the Lord... stay with the gospel and the simple verses that make the plan of salvation clear and understandable to the lost, such as John 3:16; Ephesians 2:8, 9; Acts 16:31.

CHAPTER XIV—20TH CENTURY PROTESTANTISM

Through the study of church history we discover that the majority of those Protestant churches that were started during, and as a result of, the 16th Century Reformation were formed as an effort to have and maintain pure doctrine from the Word of God in their worship.

Men such as Martin Luther were certainly great men of God, who stood firmly for the Word of God regardless of the terrible persecution they received. Ulrich Zwingli, John Calvin, and John Wesley were bold servants of the Lord who helped in leading the reform of the Christian church back to the fundamental teachings of the Word of God.

However, the doctrines taught when the various denominations were STARTED are not necessarily the doctrines taught in these same denominations today. There have been many splits branching from the main denominations, and it is difficult to correctly "label" a particular doctrine as being taught by any entire denomination for this reason.

To those churches and those pastors who have remained true to the Word of God despite the tremendous pressures put upon them by Satan, men, and organizations, we say PRAISE GOD!

It is our desire for you, as a soulwinner, to be able to recognize false doctrine whenever you hear it, and to know how to present the truth of that doctrine in an effective way. Often the errors will have a bearing on salvation, and thus are of vital importance.

It isn't our purpose to try to "knock" or degrade any particular church or denomination. Perhaps other churches bearing the same name would teach the doctrine correctly. It isn't even necessarily beneficial for you to connect automatically a certain error with a certain church, because the error may or may not be taught by a particular minister; also, the error may vary in form or degree from one church to another.

As an ambassador for Christ you should never take for granted that a person knows the Lord as his Saviour. Because he is a member of your church, a Baptist church, Methodist, Presbyterian, or Lutheran church, is no guarantee that he is saved.

In Paul's farewell address to the elders of the Ephesian church he told them, "I have not shunned to declare unto you ALL the counsel of God" (Acts 20:27). He then mentions that it is their duty, as Christian leaders, to FEED the flock and to WARN the flock, "For I know this, that after my departing shall grievous wolves enter in among you, not sparing the flock" (v. 29). If you are in the position of leadership among Christians, not only is it your responsibility to build the believers up through the Word, but it is also your divinely-appointed task to WARN those in your care of FALSE DOCTRINE.

The Apostle Peter also spoke of the danger of false doctrine, taught by false teachers: "But there were false prophets also among the people, even as there shall be false teachers among you, who privily shall bring in damnable heresies, even denying the Lord that bought them, and bring upon themselves swift destruction. And MANY shall follow their pernicious ways; by reason of whom the WAY OF TRUTH shall be evil spoken of. And through covetousness shall they with FEIGNED WORDS make merchandise of you..." (II Peter 2:1-3).

Paul warned, "Now I beseech you, brethren, MARK them which cause divisions and offenses contrary to the DOCTRINE which ye have learned; AND AVOID THEM" (Romans 16:17). You are not to: accept their sponsorship... you and your message are God-sponsored; or accept their money... God will take care of your financial needs; or have them on your platform... for what fellowship have you with Satan?; or support their schools... you would be perpetuating their errors; or send converts to their churches... babes in Christ need the WORD!

The Bible is unmistakably clear on this subject. "Be ye NOT unequally yoked together with unbelievers: for what fellowship hath righteousness with unrighteousness? And what communion hath light with darkness? And what concord hath Christ with Belial (Satan)? Or what part hath he that believeth with an infidel?" (II Cor. 6:14, 15)

This verse isn't speaking about people who don't believe in God. It is speaking of those that do not believe that God took on flesh and made a complete payment for their sin. And verse 17 says, "Wherefore come out from among them, and be ye SEPARATE, saith the Lord...."

I'm sure you know Christians who, every time they hear a new preacher, say... "My, wasn't he WONDERFUL?" The preacher may have been off on salvation, messed up the invitation, misused any number of Scriptures; yet if he was humorous, quoted from famous men, or spoke with words so large you couldn't understand what he was saying, many people would think his message was WONDERFUL. The people may have been so taken by his "sincerity and spiritual tones" or his "vivid illustrations and sentimental stories" that they did not stop to see if this man's MESSAGE was true to the Word of God!

Scripture exhorts us "That we henceforth be no more children, tossed to and fro and carried about with EVERY WIND OF DOCTRINE, by the sleight of men, and cunning craftiness, whereby they lie in wait to deceive." What is a believer to do when he hears something taught that does not "ring clear" to him? How can we know what is Scriptural and what is not?

"STUDY to shew thyself approved unto God, a workman that needeth not to be ashamed, RIGHTLY DIVIDING the Word of truth" (II Tim. 2: 15).

"All Scripture is given by inspiration of God, and is profitable for DOCTRINE, for reproof, for correction, for instruction in righteousness" (II Tim. 3:16).

Compare SCRIPTURE with SCRIPTURE, not preacher with preacher! "Knowing this first, that no prophecy of the Scripture is of any private interpretation" (II Peter 1:20). Scofield's note says this means it is "not isolated from all that the Word has given elsewhere." To understand the Bible properly, you must compare all the verses given on the subject under consideration. This takes study. As a soulwinner, you should know the Bible well enough to know IMMEDIATELY when you hear something contrary to God's plan of salvation.

"Neo-evangelicals" call those preachers who don't quite preach salvation the way the Bible says, "fringe friends." Have you read Galatians 1: 8 recently? Did it say, "But though we, or an angel from heaven preach ANY other gospel unto you than that which we have preached unto you, let him be a fringe friend"? No! God uses strong language because that is how He feels about the matter. God says, "let him be ACCURSED."

Please at this time go back to Chapter Seven and reread the reasons given for Galatianism being an accursed message.

It is a tragedy... but many Protestant churches today do not even believe the Bible is the Word of God. Some would say the Bible "becomes" the Word of God as an individual comes into "contact" with Christ. Others say the Bible "contains" the Word of God. Others come right out and admit that they do not believe the Bible is any more the Word of God than is the Koran or the Book of Mormon. They teach that any book a person finds uplifting to his soul, that book is inspired of God to him.

Around the time of 1910-1930, "Fundamentalism" or "Orthodoxy" was strong. This school stood for the Bible as the completely inerrant and inspired Word of God. R. A. Torrey, J. Gresham Machen, Robert Dick Wilson, and Benjamin Warfield-great defenders of the faith-were "Fundamentalists" of their day.

In time men arose, writing and speaking of their complete disbelief in the Bible as the Word of God, representing the left-wing, liberal theology of the day.

There was no spirit of cooperation among the "Fundamentalists" and the "Liberals" because their positions were (and are) complete opposites. The Bible tells us not to have company with those who deny the Word of God.

Today the problem seems to be with the ministers who take a position somewhere in-between the Orthodox and Liberal position. This school is called "Neo-evangelicalism."

Dr. Charles J. Woodbridge, church historian and beloved expositor of the Word, made a study of Neo-evangelicalism and gave us much of the information presented here. The following four points are taken from his lecture delivered to the Florida Bible College student body in 1963. (The reason we go into all this detail in a book on personal evangelism is that so many dear, Christian people today do not even see the dangers of this Neo-evangelicalism-they do not see that the ideas supported by it are the cause of many people being blinded to the plan of salvation.)

1. There is a new attitude of scholars. Perhaps influenced by liberalism (while they received their education), they now have an emphasis on LOVE rather than on sound DOCTRINE. This sounds beautiful, but Scripture says believers are not to make common cause with the enemy. Love is no substitute for truth.

2. There is a new method. The ministers of this school have convinced themselves that the "end justifies the means." They feel free to use any method, as long as their goal is all right. But the Scripture teaches us to act "princip'ially" (Dr. Woodbridge's coined word) and leave the results with God. We should never do evil that good may come.

Moses disobeyed God in smiting the Rock in a way not prescribed by God. Did the water come out? God overruled Moses' sin by His grace to meet the needs of the people.

Some would ask us, as they asked Dr. Woodbridge, "Don't you want to see souls saved?" And our answer is the same. OF COURSE we want to see souls saved. But we should do God's will GOD'S WAY if we are to receive God's full approval of what we are doing. Noah preached for 120 years. How many souls did he lead to the Lord? Only seven? He left the results with God–Noah's job was to preach what the Lord had TOLD him to preach.

Our responsibility is to make the gospel clear and understandable to the lost. God wants us to be FAITHFUL with His message (I Cor. 4:2). We can plant and water all we want to, but it is still God who gives the increase. Actually, "soulwinning" is a misnomer. We do not win the soul. God does this. We just give out the message.

3. There is a new theology. Those adhering to this Neo-evangelical theology often are the ones who are saying evolution and the Bible are compatible. Among them are those who deny the inspiration of II Peter, Esther, and parts of Genesis. They want to "re-define" inspiration.

As Dr. Woodbridge said, "How can you redefine 'holy men of God spake as they were moved by the Holy Ghost'? Would you say:

(1) holy means 'unholy'
(2) men means 'women'
(3) of God means 'of the devil'
(4) spake means 'sang'?" etc.

Either the Bible is the Word of God, or the Bible is a complete hoax. THERE IS NO MIDDLE GROUND!

4. There is a new ethic. It allows the people to pretty much choose their own moral system. If it makes you happy, it must be all right. The Bible says, "There is a way that seemeth right unto a man, but the end thereof are the ways of death" (Prov. 16: 25). There is no getting around "whatsoever a man soweth, that shall he also reap" (Gal. 6:7).

This Neo-evangelicalism is getting more and more popular across America today. Fewer and fewer pastors seem to realize its danger. It is fast becoming the "mode" of 20th Century Protestantism. Some independent, fundamental churches are awake. Perhaps more and more ministers within the framework of denominations will become awake... if you will faithfully give out the gospel of the Lord Jesus Christ. If you will study the Word so that you can "give an answer to every man that asketh you a reason of the hope that is in you," you will be doing much to stem the tide of Modernism.

Intricately interwoven into the fiber of modern-day Protestantism is what has become known as the Ecumenical Movement, and, as a soulwinner, you need to know how this movement is keeping the unsaved from trusting Christ as their Saviour.

The Ecumenical Movement is dangerous, first of all, because of its FALSE DOCTRINES. At the core of ecumenism is found the basic belief of the "brotherhood of man" and the "Fatherhood of God." When a person believes that all people are brothers and that God is already the Father of everyone, he does not see his need of a Saviour.

Because of this, evangelism has become "passé" to an ecumenist. In its place is substituted the "social gospel" which is aimed at improving society in general, rather than at the salvation of souls.

Another danger of ecumenism is that it CONFUSES people, even many saved people, into thinking that nothing can be really wrong that talks so much about "love" and "brotherhood." But love that leaves out TRUTH is not love. It is a counterfeit with no power to save or satisfy. Any teaching that is concerned only with man and his condition here on earth, with little or no concern for man's future destiny, is not true to God's Word and is not fulfilling Christ's last and most important command to "preach the gospel to every creature."

Avid ecumenists are growing in number throughout the various Protestant denominations and even including much of the Catholic Church. Obviously, almost 100% of these people are lost, without Christ as their personal Saviour. They are trying to do good by their brotherly kindness, and the truth of salvation by faith in Christ alone is completely foreign to them and, as they look on things, irrelevant. The spirit and doctrine of ecumenism have blinded millions into thinking "everything is fine."

Remember, anything that is contrary to the Scriptures does not find any favor with God. Don't play "patty-cake" with a movement which is against God's Word and His will. God does not need unscriptural tools or movements in His plan of evangelism. What God is looking for is a dedicated child of His who is willing to do anything or go anywhere to reach lost souls with the gospel. By His grace, let us determine to be that person.

The great need of people today, including Protestants, is a clear understanding of the gospel. The main issue in witnessing to Protestants will be grace and works. To the Protestants who are liberal in their theology, you will also need to establish the fact that the Bible is the Word of God.

Your message to most Protestants will be essentially the material given in the first two chapters of this book.

Keep your message simple. Don't take for granted that because a person goes to church he understands ecclesiastical terminology or Bible doctrine.

Start at the beginning... We are all sinners... The payment for sin is death... We must be perfect to have eternal life... We cannot earn this perfection by what we do... God offers His righteousness through the payment Christ made on the cross... Only belief in the Lord Jesus Christ will save... We can know we have eternal life once we have accepted Christ as our Saviour.

Resist the temptation to get off onto side issues and philosophical discussions. What is the power of God unto salvation to the Protestants? THE GOSPEL!

CHAPTER XV—JEHOVAH'S WITNESSES
Historical Background

(As a soulwinner, you should be familiar with the history of the various religions and cults even though you would seldom use this information during your presentation of the gospel itself.)

CHARLES TAZE RUSSELL, born February 16, 1852, was the founder of the Jehovah's Witnesses although the group was not called by that name during his lifetime.

As a young teenager, Russell belonged to the Congregational Church. He believed in and had a great fear of hell, but when he was only seventeen, a skeptic persuaded him that hell was not real. From then on, Russell fought the doctrine with all his might.

He conducted a Bible class at the age of eighteen, and when he was twenty, was made "pastor" of the group. This was the beginning of the cult. Russell set the date for the Lord's return as 1874, and he published his first piece of literature that year, entitled The Object and Manner of the Lord's Return.

Russell had some trouble in court... He was sued for divorce in 1903... His sale of "miracle wheat" which was supposed to be specially blessed was exposed in court... He committed perjury on the witness stand when a pastor, J. J. Ross, and he were in court over a pamphlet Ross wrote exposing Russell.

Russell died of cystitis in 1916.

"JUDGE" RUTHERFORD—Joseph Franklin Rutherford, born in 1869, was a lawyer member of the cult and defended Russell in his many legal suits. In January, 1917, he was chosen to succeed Russell.

During the twenty years he controlled the cult, he wrote approximately 100 books and pamphlets, which were translated into nearly 80 languages with a total distribution of over three hundred million copies.

Rutherford let Russell's books go out of print, so that today some members of the Jehovah's Witnesses do not even know of Russell and the facts regarding him.

After being called "Russellism," "Millennial Dawnism," and "International Bible Students," the cult took on its permanent name in 1931, "Jehovah's Witnesses." Rutherford claimed divine sanction of the name from Isaiah 43:10.

NATHAN H. KNORR was chosen as the new leader of the Jehovah's Witnesses at the death of Rutherford in 1942. Knorr was born in 1905 and had become a Witness at the age of sixteen.

Knorr has seen to it that all literature coming from the Watchtower Society (name of the cult's publishing headquarters) is anonymous. Rutherford's name, too, has faded, so that devotion in today's Jehovah's Witnesses movement is to the "Divine Organization" rather than to a personality.

At this writing Knorr continues as head of the cult.

The main issue in witnessing to the Jehovah's Witnesses is "grace and works." They do not believe that Jesus was God in the flesh, and they do not believe His death on the cross made a payment for all sin of those who would accept that payment by faith. They do not believe a person can KNOW he will go to heaven when he dies. They believe their life hereafter is determined by their actions on earth now.

Verses like Ephesians 2:8, 9 and Romans 4:5 are foreign to their system of theology. Making the plan of salvation understandable to them will be very difficult for you... not because you will not present it properly, but because they are often willfully blind to the gospel of God's saving grace. You can show them a clear verse of Scripture, and if they don't want to believe what it is obviously saying, they can somehow just ignore it and turn to some other verse they like better.

Jehovah's Witnesses do possess a reputation for having a great knowledge of the Bible. They certainly appear to, to the average layman. They DO know the verses in the Bible they have been TAUGHT, but very few Jehovah's Witnesses actually know the Bible very well at all from the standpoint of context or literal interpretation of clear doctrine.

The test of any group that claims to be "Christian" is its doctrines and how its doctrines compare with the clear teaching of Scripture. On some points the Jehovah's Witnesses miserably fail. Below are some of their teachings (taken from their own writings) and Scriptures showing the difference between truth and error.

Salvation According to the Jehovah's Witnesses

"The ransom does not guarantee everlasting life to any man, but only a second chance" (Truth Shall Make You Free, pp. 176, 177).

Men will be given a second chance for salvation during the millennium (Studies in the Scriptures, Vol. 1, pp. 106, 107).

"One forfeited life could redeem one forfeited life, but no more. The man Christ Jesus redeemed Adam" (ibid., p. 133).

"The second trial will decide whether we may, or may not have everlasting life" (The Watchtower, February 15, 1960, p. 143).

Salvation According to the Bible

"He that believeth on Him is not condemned: but he that believeth not is condemned already, because he hath not believed in the Name of the only begotten Son of God" (John 3:18).

"He that believeth on the Son hath everlasting life: and he that believeth not the Son shall not see life; but the wrath of God abideth on him" (John 3:36).

"Believe on the Lord Jesus Christ and thou shalt be saved" (Acts 16:31).

"Verily, verily, I say unto you, He that believeth on Me hath everlasting life" (John 6:47). Christ's own guarantee to believers.

"And as it is appointed unto men once to die, but after this the judgment" (Hebrews 9: 27). There is no second chance after death.

"For there is one God, and one mediator between God and men, the man Christ Jesus; Who gave-Himself a ransom for all..." (I Tim. 2:5, 6). Christ was not just a ransom for Adam, but a ransom for ALL!

The Christ of Jehovah's Witnesses

"He is a 'mighty God' but not the 'Almighty God who is Jehovah' " (Truth Shall Make You Free, p. 47).

"He was the first and direct creation of Jehovah God... He was the start of God's creative work" (The Kingdom Is at Hand, pp. 46-49).

Jesus Christ is Jehovah God

1. Isaiah 43:10, 11-The LORD, Jehovah, says, "... before Me there was no God formed, neither shall there be after Me." The LORD, Jehovah, says, "... beside Me there is no Saviour." (See Isa. 44:6, 8; Deut. 4:39.)

Therefore, if Christ is God in any way, if Christ is the Saviour in any way, then according to the LORD God Jehovah, Christ is GOD.

Luke 2: 11 says, "For unto you is born this day in the city of David a Saviour, which is Christ the Lord."

Since Christ is the Saviour, then Christ is GOD.

2. Isaiah 42:8-"I am the LORD: that is My Name: and My glory will I not give to another...."

Only Jehovah God is the LORD of glory. If Christ is the Lord of glory, then He must be Jehovah God.

I Cor. 2:8 says the crucified Christ is the "Lord of glory." Since Christ is the Lord of glory, then Christ is GOD.

3. Zechariah 12:1-10-The LORD, Jehovah, says, "... and they shall look upon Me whom they have pierced...."

When was the Lord, Jehovah, pierced?

"But when they came to Jesus, and saw that He was dead already, they brake not His legs: But one of the soldiers with a spear pierced His side, and forthwith came there out blood and water. And he that saw it bare record, and his record is true: and he knoweth that he saith true, that ye might believe. For these things were done, that the Scripture should be fulfilled, A bone of Him shall not be broken, and again another Scripture saith, They shall look on Him whom they pierced" (John 19:33-37).

Since Christ was pierced, and Jehovah God said He would be pierced, then Christ is God.

4. Isaiah 7:14-"Therefore the Lord Himself shall give you a sign; Behold, a virgin shall conceive, and bear a son, and shall call His Name Immanuel."

Read Matt. 1:18-25. Notice in v. 18, the child was "OF the Holy Ghost..." and Mary was with child "BEFORE they (Mary and Joseph) came together." Again, in v. 20 the angel of the Lord confirms the child is "OF the Holy Ghost." In v. 21 the child shall be named JESUS because He shall save His people from their sins. The very name Jesus means "God who saves," etc. And in vv. 22, 23, we learn that "all this was done that it might be fulfilled which was spoken OF THE LORD by the prophet, saying, Behold, a virgin shall be with child, and shall bring forth a son, and they shall call His Name Emmanuel, which being interpreted is, GOD WITH US."

So God Himself says the child Jesus is actually GOD HIMSELF dwelling with man. This is again clearly confirmed in John 1:1-14. "The Word was God... And the Word was made flesh and dwelt among us...."

5. Mark 2:5 records that Jesus forgave people's sins. The scribes heard Christ doing this and said (v. 7), "Why doth this man thus speak blasphemies? Who can forgive sins but GOD ONLY?" They failed to realize that Christ wasn't doing anything blasphemous at all. HE WAS GOD!

6. Luke 1:68 records at the time of the birth of Christ, "Blessed be the LORD GOD of Israel; for He hath visited and redeemed His people."

7. Luke 8: 39-Christ had just cast out demons and told the person, "Return to thine own house and shew how great things GOD hath done unto thee. And he went his way, and published throughout the whole city how great things JESUS had done unto him."

This is not a contradiction. Christ did it and said God did it. Christ told the man to say God did it and the man said Christ did it. It is not a contradiction because Christ is GOD.

8. In John 9:33-38 is recorded Christ's conversation with a man who wanted to know who Christ was. Christ said He was the Son of God and the man (v. 38) "worshiped Him." Christ did not reprove this man for worshipping Him, and yet Christ knew the clear commands of the Old Testament not to worship any God but Jehovah God. Exodus 34: 14, "For thou shalt worship no other god; for the LORD, whose name is Jealous, is a jealous God."

If Christ were not truly God and accepted the worship from a man without even rebuking the man, then Christ would not even have been an honest man.

Christ did accept worship. For Christ is GOD. (See John 5:23.)

9. John 14: 7-Christ says, "If ye had known Me, ye should have known My Father also: and from henceforth ye know Him and have seen Him," and vv. 8, 9, "Philip saith unto Him, Lord, shew us the Father, and it sufficeth us. Jesus saith unto him, Have I been so long time with you, and yet hast thou not known Me, Philip? He that hath seen ME HATH SEEN THE FATHER: and how sayest thou then, Shew us the Father?" (See John 12:45.)

In John 15:24 Christ again says people have "both seen and hated both Me and My Father."

The reason Christ can say that when someone has seen Him he has also seen the Father is that Christ is GOD, one and the same as the Father.

10. John 10:30-33 tells us the same thing. Christ said in v. 30, "I and My Father are ONE." And "Then the Jews took up stones again to stone Him" (v. 31). In answer to Christ's questions of why they were stoning Him they replied in verse 33, "... for blasphemy; and because that thou, being a man, makest thyself God."

The Jews KNEW Christ was claiming to be God. They were so sure of His claims that they wanted to stone Him for what they SUPPOSED to be blasphemy.

But Christ didn't commit blasphemy. Even a good, godly human being would know better than to commit blasphemy, time after time, especially when he was constantly being accused of it.

Christ could say "I and My Father are One" because it is true. Christ is GOD.

11. Acts 20:28 says, "... to feed the church of God, which He hath purchased with His own blood."

When did God shed His blood? God shed His blood when He took on flesh in the person of Jesus Christ and shed His blood for our sins. Christ said in Luke 22:20, "... This cup is the new testament in My blood, which is shed for you." Revelation 1:5 says, "And from Jesus Christ, who is the faithful witness, and the first begotten of the dead, and the prince of the kings of the earth. Unto Him that loved us, and washed us from our sins in His own blood."

God shed His blood when Jesus shed His blood because Jesus is GOD.

12. Ezekiel 44:2-"Then said the LORD unto me; This gate shall be shut, it shall not be opened, and no man shall enter in by it; because the LORD, the God of Israel, hath entered in by it, therefore it shall be shut."

This is the gate that the LORD God, the LORD JESUS CHRIST, entered at His "triumphal entry" spoken of in John 12: 12-16 and each of the other Gospels. The Mohammedans closed the gate soon after the destruction of the Temple in 70 A.D., and it shall remain shut.

13. In John 12:26 Christ says, "... if any man serve Me (Christ), him will My Father honour." And yet in Matt. 4:10 Christ affirms the Old Testament command, "Thou shalt worship the Lord thy God and HIM ONLY shalt thou serve."

Christ, knowing and upholding the Old Testament teaching, would not tell people to serve Him, and would not tell people God the Father would honor their lives when they do serve Him... in direct contradiction to the command in the Old Testament to serve only the LORD THY GOD.

Man is honored by God the Father when man serves Christ because Christ is GOD.

14. Rev. 15:3, 4-"... Great and marvellous are Thy works, LORD GOD ALMIGHTY; just and true are Thy ways, Thou King of saints. Who shall not fear Thee, O Lord, and glorify Thy Name? For Thou ONLY art holy."

But Luke 1:35 records the words of the angel Gabriel, who was sent from God, saying, "... that HOLY thing which shall be born of thee shall be called the Son of God."

Only the Lord God Almighty is holy... but the Son of God is holy because He IS the Lord God Almighty.

15. Genesis 1:1 says, "God created the heaven and the earth." Hebrews 1:2 and Colossians 1:15-17 say Christ created it.

16. Titus 3: 4 says "God our Saviour." Titus 3: 6 says "Jesus Christ our Saviour." Isaiah 43: 11 says the LORD (Jehovah) is the ONLY Saviour.

Do these three verses contradict? No! But they WOULD contradict if Jesus Christ and Jehovah God weren't one and the same.

17. I John 5: 20 calls Christ "the true God." Hebrews 1: 8 refers to the Son of God as "O God." In Rev. 1: 8 Christ is speaking (see v. 5) and says He is the "Alpha and Omega, the beginning and the ending, saith the Lord, which is, and which was, and which is to come, the ALMIGHTY."

18. Colossians 2:9-"For in Him (Christ, v. 8) dwelleth all the fullness of the Godhead bodily." Everything that is in the Godhead, everything that is God, was in Christ in a bodily form. "For it pleased the Father that IN HIM (Christ) should all fulness dwell" (Col. 1: 19).

19. I Timothy 3:16-"And without controversy great is the mystery of godliness: God was manifest in the flesh, (GOD was) justified in the Spirit, (GOD was) seen of angels, (GOD was) preached unto the Gentiles, (GOD was) believed on in the world, (GOD was) received up into glory."

When did this happen? When Jesus Christ was manifest in the flesh, justified in the Spirit, seen of angels, preached unto the Gentiles, believed on in the world, and received up into glory.

The Bible says, "God was manifest in the flesh," etc., because Christ is GOD.

20. In Romans 10:9 and 13 the Apostle Paul quoted from an Old Testament prophet saying, "For whosoever shall call upon the Name of the Lord shall be saved." Of course, Paul was speaking of Jesus as Lord (Rom. 10:9). But the verse he was quoting in the Old Testament is Joel 2:32 which says, "... whosoever shall call on the Name of the LORD (Jehovah) shall be delivered (saved)."

Why did the Holy Spirit give the Apostle Paul the liberty to use an Old Testament verse which speaks of JEHOVAH and apply it to the LORD JESUS CHRIST? Because the Lord Jesus Christ is Jehovah.

21. Isaiah 9:6 prophesies of the Messiah to come, "For unto us a child is born, unto us a son is given: and the government shall be upon His shoulder: and His Name shall be called Wonderful, Counsellor, the Mighty God, the EVERLASTING FATHER, The Prince of Peace."

Our Messiah, the Lord Jesus Christ, is the Everlasting Father.

22. Micah 5:2, also prophesying of the coming Messiah, says, "whose goings forth have been from of old, FROM EVERLASTING."

But Psalm 90:2 says, "Before the mountains were brought forth, or ever thou hadst formed the earth and the world, even from EVERLASTING to everlasting, thou art GOD."

Christ was from everlasting, was in existence and one with God before the world was formed (John 17:5) because Christ is GOD.

23. When Moses asked God, "Behold, when I come unto the children of Israel, and shall say unto them, The God of your fathers hath sent me unto you; and they shall say to me, What is His name? What shall I say unto them?" (Exod. 3:13) God answered unto Moses (v. 14), "I AM THAT I AM: and He said, Thus shalt thou say unto the children of Israel, I AM hath sent me unto you."

Christ, revealing Himself unto the Jewish people, made this life and death statement unto them in John 8:24, "I said therefore unto you, that ye shall die in your sins: for if ye believe not that I AM (he), ye shall die in your sins."

To be saved, a person must believe that the Lord Jesus Christ was truly God Himself, who gave His life to make a death and blood payment for his sin, which He did. "For the wages of sin is death; but the gift of God is eternal life through Jesus Christ OUR LORD" (Romans 6:23). (Reprinted from booklet, Jesus Christ Is Jehovah God, distributed by Soul Winning Seminars, 6/67.)

The Trinity Disbelieved by Witnesses

"There is no authority in the Word of God for the doctrine of the Trinity of the Godhead" (Studies in the Scriptures, Vol. 5, pp. 54-60). "... Satan is the originator of the 'trinity' doctrine" (Let God Be True, 1946 ed., p. 82).

The Trinity Taught in Scripture

The Father is God: II Timothy 1:2; I Thessalonians 1:1.

The Holy Spirit is God: Acts 5:1-4; Isa. 48:16; Job 33:4; Isa. 63:7-10.

The Son, Jesus Christ, is God: See list on preceding pages.

Matthew 28:19 says, "Go ye therefore, and teach all nations, baptizing them in the NAME (singular in the Greek) of the Father, and of the Son, and of the Holy Ghost." If there were three gods, or if one were God, and one were a created being, and the other were just God's "power" (as the J. W.'s say), then the verse would have to say to baptize in the "names" of the Father, Son, and Holy Ghost.

God is very exact and lets us know in this verse that though there is only one God, He is a triune God.

Even in Deuteronomy 6:4, where it says that "Our God is one LORD (Jehovah)," the Trinity is proven. In Hebrew there are at least two words translated "one." The word "one" in this verse is "echod" and means "a unity." The Hebrew word "yachid" is the word meaning "an absolute one." The word translated "God" in the Hebrew is "Elohim" and means three or more. God says precisely what He means.

Man According to the Witnesses

Man is a soul, but does not have a soul (Let God Be True, p. 60).

"... the serpent (the Devil) is the one who originated the doctrine of the inherent immortality of the soul" (ibid., p. 66).

Man According to God

"I pray God your whole spirit AND SOUL and body be preserved blameless unto the coming of our Lord Jesus Christ" (I Thess. 5:23).

"Beloved, I wish above all things that thou mayest prosper and be in health, even as thy soul prospereth" (III John, v. 2).

Man was created in God's image (Genesis 1:26), a triune being, having body, soul, and spirit. And the Bible says, "The Word of God is quick, and powerful, and sharper than any two-edged sword, piercing even to the dividing asunder of SOUL, and SPIRIT, and of the JOINTS and MARROW (body)..." (Heb. 4:12).

Death and Hell as Taught by the Watchtower Society

The penalty of the second chance for life will be the second death, which is annihilation (Studies in the Scriptures, Vol. 1, p. 151).

God is too good to sustain an everlasting hell (ibid., p. 127).

"The grave and physical death are the only hell" (Reconciliation, p. 289).

"The doctrine of eternal torment is as false as its author, the devil" (Creation, p. 341).

"It is so plain that the Bible hell is the tomb, the grave, that even an honest little child can understand it, but not the religious theologians" (Let God Be True, p. 72).

Death and Hell as Taught by the Bible

"And these shall go away into EVERLASTING PUNISHMENT (not annihilation): but the righteous into life eternal" (Matt. 25:46).

"Even as Sodom and Gomorrah, and the cities about them in like manner, giving themselves over to fornication, and going after strange flesh, are set forth for an example, suffering the vengeance of ETERNAL FIRE" (Jude, v. 7). Obviously, it is the PEOPLE in these cities that will suffer. (Cities do not "commit fornication," but the people IN the cities.)

"And the smoke of their torment ascendeth up FOR EVER AND EVER; and they have no rest day nor night, who worship the beast and his image, and whosoever receiveth the mark of his name" (Rev. 14:11).

Luke 16:24, "... for I am tormented in this flame."

Luke 16:26, "... there is a great gulf fixed, so that they which would pass from hence to you cannot; neither can they pass to us, that would come from thence.?"

Luke 16:28, "... lest they also come into this place of torment."

Daniel 12:2, "And many of them that sleep in the dust of the earth shall awake, some to everlasting life, and some to shame and everlasting contempt."

Suggestions for Your Witnessing

(1) Be courteous and patient. One of the things Jehovah's Witnesses seem to delight in is being persecuted. It is supposed to be some kind of proof that they are God's true servants. When you are rude or abrupt with them it confirms in their minds that they really must be the "true sheep" of the Lord. This makes it that much harder for the next Christian to witness to them. Don't argue. Firmly point out the truth in the Scriptures.

(2) Somewhere in the beginning of your conversation get the Witness to agree to talk only about what is important... like salvation. You might say, "Being human, we are bound to disagree on some small points. So why don't we confine our talk to really important subjects like how to be saved?" He will almost always agree to this.

This will help you tremendously. Every time he tries to go off on some side issue, you can politely remind him of the agreement and bring the conversation back to the gospel. In this way you will have a much greater chance of leading him to Christ.

(3) Be an attentive listener. The best soulwinners listen carefully to what the other person is saying so they can catch things they will want to utilize in their witnessing.

(4) Ask questions. It is important to ask the Witness what he means by certain phrases. For instance, what he means by "ransom sacrifice," Christ being the "Son of God," and "death," etc., is often completely different from what you mean.

Often his words sound Biblical, but what he means is unscriptural. In order to combat the error you must know what the error is, and many times the error is not apparent on the surface.

(5) Perhaps even more than with other people, you need to USE THE BIBLE to win them. The Witnesses are under the impression that they are the only ones who really know the Bible. The truth is, they usually do not know the Bible very well... only certain "proof texts" which they can readily produce. However, most Protestants (and many born-again believers) don't usually know as much of God's Word as the Jehovah's Witnesses do. Therefore, when they are speaking to someone they always speak as the teacher, assuming that the listener knows nothing of the Bible.

They are shocked to find someone who knows as much or more than they. However, although it is extremely important to use God's Word as you witness to them, be careful of trying to show them how much you know by using TOO MANY verses. It is almost always best to use as few verses as possible... clear ones... and stay with them.

(6) Keep in mind that the average Jehovah's Witness is like "quicksilver." When you show him a verse he doesn't like or doesn't have an answer for, he will want to jump over to some other passage. Often that passage will be off the subject of salvation. DON'T LET HIM DO THIS. Stay on the passage you are showing him until he either admits what the verse is saying, or he admits he does not believe the verse. This is almost impossible for you to do, but strive for it.

(7) If, after all your best efforts to get him to understand the plan of salvation, he still refuses to accept Christ as his Saviour, DON'T LET HIM LEAVE FEELING COMFORTABLE. This advice goes for any lost person you speak with but especially the Witness, who is so sure that there is no hell to worry about.

(8) A closing remark to an unbelieving Witness might be, "If what you believe is true, and I don't believe it, all I must face is being annihilated. But if what the Bible says about hell is true, and you don't believe it and accept Christ as your Saviour, you face an eternity in the lake of fire." Let him know that neither you nor God wants him to go to hell. Speak the truth in love.

CHAPTER XVI—Seventh-Day Adventism

Historical Background

William Miller is the forerunner of Seventh-Day Adventism, although the person most identified with the movement is Ellen G. White.

In 1818 Miller, a New England farmer, predicted Christ was coming again on March 21, 1843. (This date was decided upon by interpreting the 2300 days of the prophecy in Daniel 8:14 as years and adding 2300 years to 457 B.C.) Of course, Christ did not return that year.

The date was changed to October 24, 1844. Again, Christ did not appear. Miller was bitterly disappointed. Before his death in 1849 he even said, "We expected the personal coming of Christ at that time; and now to contend that we were not mistaken is dishonest. We should never be ashamed frankly to confess our errors. I have no confidence in any of the new theories that grew out of the movement..." (Good News Broadcaster, June, 1964).

However, many who followed Miller started their own groups, and one of them became the foundation of modern Seventh-Day Adventism. Ellen G. White was one of the leaders of this group. Instead of admitting a mistake in calculation as Miller had done, this group insisted that Christ had come in 1844. They said instead of coming back to the earth, He entered the "Heavenly Sanctuary" to (supposedly) finish the atonement and that when Christ is through with the atonement, He will come the rest of the way to the earth. (See Heb. 10: 12-the atonement is finished!)

Mrs. White did a lot of writing. Among her books are The Desire of the Ages, Patriarchs and Prophets, The Acts of the Apostles, Prophets and Kings, and a very popular booklet, Steps to Christ. This booklet has had a distribution of millions. The attitude of those who follow her is that there are no errors in her writings. However, not all Adventists concede that she is a prophet in the same sense as Isaiah, Jeremiah, etc.

Some Christian leaders of our day are saying that modern Adventism has departed enough from its original view that it should not be considered "heresy." If its errors were completely on minor points, we might tend to agree with them. However, since it puts works into salvation, we have no other choice than to point out that such teaching is definitely unscriptural.

Brief Doctrinal Coverage of Adventism

Questions on Doctrine, 1957, says that Ellen G. White's book The Great Controversy is "one of our standard books." In this book are found many doctrines strange to the Word of God.

Salvation

Mrs. White says, "As the books of record are opened in the judgment, the lives of all who have believed in Jesus come in review before God... Every name is mentioned, every case closely investigated. Names are accepted, names rejected. When any have sins remaining upon the books of record, unrepented of and unforgiven, their names will be blotted out of the book of life, and the record of their good deeds will be erased... All who have truly repented of sin, AND by faith claimed the blood of Christ as their atoning sacrifice, have had pardon entered against their names in the books of heaven; as they have become partakers of the righteousness of Christ, and their characters are found to be in harmony with the law of God, their sins will be blotted out, and they themselves will be accounted WORTHY of eternal life" (The Great Controversy, p. 483).

According to this statement of Mrs. White's, even though one "believes on Jesus" he will still be lost if he dies with any sins on his record that he had not repented of. But if a person believes in Jesus AND his character is good, God will give him what he has EARNED through his faith and worthy deeds...eternal life.

Remember that Romans 11:6 tells us if a person is saved by grace then he CANNOT be saved by works also. Grace means "mercy," and if you work for something and receive a wage for it, that wage is not given to you out of mercy: It is given to you because it is owed to you... you deserve it (Romans 4:4, 5). But NO MAN DESERVES SALVATION. God does not owe man anything! We deserve hell, but God in grace gives eternal life to those who trust in Christ and His payment for all their sin. Eternal life does not come to us through faith AND "worthy deeds." It doesn't come through faith AND anything. It comes through FAITH ALONE in Christ's finished work for us. What passage in Galatians comes to your mind when you hear of someone trying to be saved by grace and works of the law? Galatians 5:1-4.

"As the priest, in removing the sins from the sanctuary, confessed them upon the head of the scapegoat, so Christ will place all these sins upon Satan, the originator and instigator of sin... Satan, bearing the guilt of all the sins which he has caused... will at last suffer the full penalty of sin in the fires that shall destroy all the wicked" (ibid., pp. 485, 486).

But God's Word plainly states, "The Lord hath laid on Him (CHRIST) the iniquity of us all" (Isaiah 53:6). CHRIST is the One who has been "made sin for us" (II Cor. 5:21). Since all of our sins were placed upon Christ, what need is there for any other sinbearer? This doctrine is blasphemy!

SOUL-SLEEP

Adventists teach that the unsaved will be annihilated and not spend eternity in the lake of fire as the Scriptures teach. Neither do they believe that a person has any consciousness

after death. This belief is called "soul-sleep" and contradicts precious Scripture on behalf of the believers who have gone home to be with the Lord. See I Thess. 4:17; II Cor. 5:6-8; Phil. 1:21, 23; Rev. 6:9, 10; and Psalm 116:15.

THE SABBATH

The unique issue among Adventists is their teaching that one must keep the Sabbath (Saturday) to be saved. This again is the issue: Are you saved by LAW or GRACE?

Any of the following Scriptures answer this, and you should learn to apply them to any issue such as this as you witness. Keeping the Sabbath or any other "work of the law" has nothing to do with salvation.

"Be it known unto you, therefore, men and brethren, that through this man is preached unto you the forgiveness of sins: and by Him ALL THAT BELIEVE are justified from all things, from which YE COULD NOT be justified by the law of Moses" (Acts 13:38, 39).

"Therefore by the deeds of the law there shall no flesh be justified in His sight: for by the law is the knowledge of sin.... Therefore we conclude that a man is justified by faith WITHOUT the deeds of the law" (Romans 3:20, 28).

"For as many as are of the works of the law are under the curse; for it is written, Cursed is every one that continueth not in ALL things which are written in the book of the law to do them. But that no man is justified by the law in the sight of God, it is evident: for, the just shall live by faith. AND THE LAW IS NOT OF FAITH..." (Gal. 3: 10-12).

"Is the law then against the promises of God? God forbid: for if there had been a law given which could have given life, verily righteousness should have been by the law. But the Scripture hath concluded all under sin, that the PROMISE BY FAITH of Jesus Christ might be GIVEN TO THEM THAT BELIEVE" (Gal. 3:21, 22).

If they want to keep the law to be saved, how much would they have to keep? They would have to keep the WHOLE law, because if they failed in just one point they would then be sinners, and have the results of sin-death (James 2:10; Rom. 6:23).

Christ asked a pointed question in John 7:19, "Did not Moses give you the law, and yet NONE of you keepeth the law?"

It is rather foolish to try to keep the law to be saved, or to try to keep the law after you are saved SO THAT you will stay saved. "Are ye so foolish? Having begun in the Spirit, are ye now made perfect by the flesh?" (Gal. 3:3)

Regarding the Sabbath, God says, "One man esteemeth one day above another: another esteemeth every day alike. Let every man be fully persuaded in his own mind" (Romans 14:5). God doesn't give the power to the local church to tell you that you must observe a particular day above an other.

"Let no man (even Seventh-Day Adventist) therefore judge you in meat, or in drink, or in respect of an holy day, or of the new moon, or OF THE SABBATH..." (Col. 2: 16).

Agree with them that Saturday is the Sabbath, the seventh day, because it is. The Sabbath has never been changed from the seventh day. But the day one chooses to worship God is not really the issue. You should worship the Lord EVERY day. How one is saved is the important point. Incidentally, the Sabbath was given as a day of REST, not as a day of WORSHIP. When the Adventists go to meetings on Saturday, they are DOING much more and TRAVELING much more than the laws governing the Sabbath allow!

If the Adventists followed the punishment Scripture attaches to disobedience of the Sabbath as prescribed by law, they would soon exterminate themselves. See Numbers 15: 32-36 and Exodus 35:2.

Christians worship on Sunday because the Apostles did, Acts 20:7; and the Apostles did because Christ rose from the dead on the first day of the week, Luke 24: 1.

Suggestions for Your Witnessing

(1) Be cautious of the subtle approach used by the Adventists to lure the unsuspecting public through their radio program, "The Voice of Prophecy," and their telecast, "Faith for Today." You can listen to or watch these programs without ever hearing of the false doctrine taught by the Seventh-Day Adventists. When you read their literature, the difference between their beliefs and the Bible is more obvious.

(2) At Christmas season a truck full of carolers may ride down your street. As they sing the beautiful songs of Christmas, nice, clean-looking young people will come to your door asking for contributions for missionary hospital work being carried on throughout the world. They are Seventh-Day Adventists, but you would never know it. They don't tell you, and neither can you discover who printed the beautiful literature they leave with you... it doesn't say. Sometimes way down on the bottom of a page in very small letters you might see three letters: SDA.

The Seventh-Day Adventists really do much good in maintaining hospitals and schools and promoting high morals. This is one reason people fail to see that it is a dangerous "religion." They see the good works of their members and assume it must be a good religion. As a soul winner, remember the teaching of II Cor. 11: 13-15, that Satan's ministers OFTEN promote "righteousness." More people are "sucked into it" that way.

(3) The Southern Publishing Company in Nashville, Tennessee, and the Review and Herald Publishing Company in Washington, D.C., are their publishing houses. Southern puts out a ten-volume set called the Bible Story, especially for children, you should be aware of.

(4) When witnessing to an Adventist, remember that INDIVIDUAL members of the church may not believe everything taught by the group as a whole. Some, no doubt, know the Lord as their Saviour... through God honoring a portion of the Word they perhaps have heard. You need to question each one to determine what he is trusting in to take him to heaven. Invariably you will find that you must go over SIMPLE verses on salvation, especially those that point out that salvation is purely by grace apart from any works or lawkeeping (Romans 4:5; 3:28; 11:6; Eph. 2:8, 9; Titus 3: 5).

(5) The official teaching (and general belief among the members) is that you cannot be sure of salvation now, and that though you may be saved now, you might lose your salvation before you die. In other words, they do not believe the gift of God is ETERNAL LIFE (Rom. 6:23). You may have to go over this truth again and again before they see it. Refer to Chapter Two for more on eternal security.

(6) No matter how hard they try to turn the conversation from the gospel to the Sabbath, etc., you must keep the conversation on the gospel. The gospel is good news, especially to those people who have been under the burden of thinking they have to keep the law to be saved.

"Walk in wisdom toward them that are without, redeeming the time. Let your speech be always with grace, seasoned with salt, that ye may know how ye ought to answer every man" (Col. 4:5, 6).

CHAPTER XVII—Christian Science and Unity

Historical Background (Christian Science)

The founder of this group was Mary Baker Glover Patterson Eddy. She was born on July 16, 1821, in Bow, New Hampshire, and was the youngest of six children. She was raised in a family of strict Calvinism but was never won to this belief herself.

Her health was very poor; it interrupted her formal education. She was a semi-invalid for years.

George Glover, whom she married in 1843, was the first of her three husbands. In less than a year after their marriage he died, leaving her with an unborn child. Later, after the death of her mother and remarriage of her father, she married Daniel Patterson. Patterson was captured and imprisoned during the Civil War. When he returned, he ran off with a neighbor's wife. Eventually he and Mary were divorced. During all these years she constantly suffered from one thing or another.

While still married to Patterson, Mary heard of Phineas Quimby, who supposedly cured people without the use of medicines. She went to see Quimby when she was 41 years old, and during several weeks at his Portland, Maine, office she received relief which she attributed to God working through Quimby. Quimby denied, however, that God had anything to do with it or that he had any special healing powers.

Mr. Quimby died in 1866 when Mary was 45 years old. Mary Baker Patterson began to portray herself as a healer from this time on. Shortly after Quimby's death she fell on an icy street and injured herself. She claimed that the doctor who examined her injury declared it to be fatal (though the physician's own testimony later on denied this). Some friends came to visit her before her supposedly impending death. She had them all leave the room while she read Matthew 9. While reading this portion of Scripture she was immediately and completely healed (so she said).

She began a school to teach others to heal, charging from $100 to $300 for a course lasting three weeks. During this time, too, she worked on her book, Science and Health with Key to the Scriptures, which later became the textbook for the cult. When the book was ready for publication, she had to get the help of her followers to print it for no Boston publisher would.

She was married the third time to Asa G. Eddy. In 1878 she organized and pastored the First Church of Christ Scientist with 26 members. During this period Mr. Eddy died of a bad heart. However, Mrs. Eddy declared he had died by "arsenic poison mentally administered" by their enemies.

Her later life was filled with sickness and nervousness. She died in 1910. Even though she claimed not to believe in the reality of death, she had to keep that appointment which God says every man must keep (Hebrews 9:27).

Christian Science Doctrine Contrasted with the Word of God, the Bible

"Genesis 2:7. Is this addition to His creation real or unreal? Is it the truth, or is it a lie concerning man and God? IT MUST BE A LIE, for God presently curses the ground" (Science and Health, p. 524).

"The second chapter of Genesis CONTAINS A STATEMENT of this material view of God and the universe, a statement WHICH IS THE EXACT OPPOSITE OF SCIENTIFIC TRUTH..." (ibid., p. 521).

"ALL Scripture is given by inspiration of God..." (II Tim. 3:16).

"In hope of eternal life, which GOD, THAT CANNOT LIE, promised before the world began" (Titus 1:2).

"Heaven and earth shall pass away, but my words shall not pass away" (Matt. 24:35).

Christ's Death for Sin

"One sacrifice, however great, is insufficient to pay the debt of sin" (Science and Health, p. 23).

"That God's wrath should be vented upon His beloved Son, is divinely unnatural" (ibid., p. 23).

"The material blood of Jesus was no more efficacious to cleanse from sin when it was shed upon 'the accursed tree' than when it was flowing in his veins as he went daily about his Father's business" (ibid., p. 25).

"For BY ONE OFFERING He hath perfected for ever them that are sanctified" (Hebrews 10:14).

"In whom we have REDEMPTION THROUGH HIS BLOOD, the forgiveness of sins, according to the riches of His grace" (Ephesians 1: 7). "All we like sheep have gone astray; we have turned every one to his own way; and the LORD HATH LAID ON HIM the iniquity of us all... it PLEASED THE LORD to bruise Him" (Isaiah 53:6, 10).

SIN

"Man is incapable of sin, sickness, and death" (Science and Health, p. 475).

"To put down the claim of sin, you must detect it, remove the mask, point out the illusion, and thus get the victory over sin and so prove its unreality" (ibid., p. 447).

"For ALL HAVE SINNED, and come short of the glory of God" (Rom. 3:23).

"For there is not a just man upon earth, that doeth good, and SINNETH NOT" (Eccl. 7:20).

THE PERSON OF JESUS CHRIST

"The virgin-mother conceived this idea of God, and gave to her ideal the name of Jesus-that is, Joshua, or Saviour" (Science and Health, p. 29).

"Jesus was the offspring of Mary's self-conscious communion with God" (ibid., pp. 29, 30).

The angel, not Mary, said, "For unto you is born this day in the city of David a SAVIOUR, which is Christ the Lord" (Luke 2:11).

"And Paul... reasoned with them out of the Scriptures, opening and alleging that Christ must needs have suffered and risen again from the dead; and that THIS JESUS, whom I preach unto you, IS CHRIST" (Acts 17:2, 3).

"... for that which is conceived in her is of the Holy Ghost... Now all this was done, that it might be fulfilled which was spoken of the Lord by the prophet, saying, Behold, a virgin shall be with child, and shall bring forth a son, and they shall call His Name Emmanuel, which being interpreted is, GOD WITH US" (Matt. 1:20, 22, 23).

"And, behold, thou shalt conceive in thy womb (not in her mind), and bring forth a son, and shalt call His Name Jesus" (Luke 1: 31).

THOUGHTS ON YOUR APPROACH

(1) You must understand the major premise or formula of the Christian Scientist in order to reach him intelligently for the Lord. His basic approach to God, salvation, etc., can be summed up in this way:

God is Love... God is Life... God is Good... God is Spirit... God is ALL. (These are all true except for the last.)

Since God is Love and God is ALL, there can be no hate. Since God is Life and God is ALL, there can be no death. Since God is Good and God is ALL, there can be no evil. Since God is Spirit and God is ALL,.there can be no matter. (So they feel there will be no hatred, illness, sin, death, etc., to the person who knows God aright.)

This is another form of "pantheism," the doctrine or belief that God is not a personality, but that all laws, forces, manifestations, etc., are God. It is strongly adhered to by Christian Scientists. This formula governs nearly all their thinking. Therefore, you need to know how to answer it from Scripture.

(2) SCRIPTURES REFUTING THE IDEA THAT "GOD IS ALL."

Genesis 1: 1, "In the beginning God CREATED the heaven and the earth." Notice it doesn't say God IS the heaven and the earth-but He created it.

Isaiah 59: 2, "Your iniquities have SEPARATED between you and your God, and your sins have hid His face from you...." Again, the truth that God is SEPARATE FROM His creation.

Numbers 23:19, "God is NOT A MAN, that He should lie...." Man lies; God does not. No thinking person really believes God is EVERYTHING!

(3) The most important thing to remember is that you must give the Christian Scientist the GOSPEL. Often a person is attracted to this cult because he doesn't want to believe that he is accountable for the sins he has committed. Christian Science gives a convenient way out for such a person and provides a FALSE sense of security. If he understood the gospel, that God loves sinners and has already made a complete payment for sin, he would perhaps respond and accept Christ as his Saviour.

(4) One reason so many elderly people are Christian Scientists is that they fear death and what lies beyond, and they do not know the love of God. The teachings of Christian Science that there is really no sin or death, etc., calm their fears.

(5) As a group, you will find that the Christian Scientists are lovely people who are trying to live the best kind of life they know how. Even though the plan of salvation excludes man's good works for entrance into heaven, there is no reason why you shouldn't compliment a person who is obviously trying to live a good life.

(6) Since the Christian Scientist doesn't believe he is a "sinner," an effective way to get across to him the truth that he needs a payment for what he has done wrong is to ask, "Are you perfect?" Most people quite readily admit that they are not perfect. When they see this and that they need to be perfect to enter heaven, half your "battle" is won.

(7) Be sure to emphasize Scriptures like John 3: 16, that point out the great LOVE God has for us, since this will be especially appealing to the Christian Scientist. The gospel-the good news that God has made a payment for sin- is the power God will use to save the Christian Scientist.

Note: "... keep that which is committed to thy trust (the gospel), avoiding profane and vain babblings, and oppositions of SCIENCE falsely so called, which some professing have ERRED concerning the faith" (I Timothy 6: 20, 21).

Historical Background (Unity)

Unity was founded in Kansas City, Missouri, in 1889 by Charles and Myrtle Fillmore. At the time, the Fillmores were almost penniless; Charles suffered from numerous ailments, including a withered leg (the result of a childhood skating accident); Mrs. Fillmore had tuberculosis.

They heard a Dr. Weeks speak on "New Thought." After the lecture Mrs. Fillmore reasoned that since we are all children of God (error), there must be a fixed divine law operating in her life. If she had faith in this law, surely all the negative things of life, like sickness and poverty, would vanish.

After this "discovery" the couple improved in health and financial status. They felt their theory had been proven. In 1889 they decided to devote the rest of their lives to spreading the gospel of their "discovery." Thus "The Unity School of Christianity" began.

Doctrines of Unity and the Truth from the Scriptures

(1) Reincarnation of man. Hebrews 9:27; Romans 5:12; Hebrews 10:30, 31.

(2) God never performs miracles. John 2: 1—11; John 6:2; Acts 2:22; Acts 15:12.

(3) Man is part of God. We may all be like Christ now. Isa. 53:6; Isa. 64:6; Romans 3:10-18, 23; Numbers 23:19.

(4) There is no evil. Genesis 6:5; John 8:39-45.

(5) Heaven and hell are states of mind. John 14:1-3; II Cor. 5:1, 2; Jude, verse 7; Matthew 25:41.

(6) Pain, sickness, poverty, old age, and death are not real. Heb. 9:27; Rom. 5:17, 18; Rom. 8:18-23; Matt. 4: 23, 24.

(7) The entire Bible is allegory. John 17: 17; Psalm 19:9-11; Psalm 119: 128, 142.

With such people as these, keep Paul's instructions to servants of the Lord in mind: "The servant of the Lord must not strive; but be gentle unto all men, apt (able) to teach, patient, in meekness instructing those that oppose them selves" (II Timothy 2:24, 25).

Thoughts on your Approach

(1) Unity's method of interpreting the Bible is "spiritualization." For instance, according to Unity, "Jerusalem" is not a city at all; it "signifies the heart centre of the individual consciousness." Peter was a "fisherman" which is "symbolical of a consciousness that is open to and seeking for new ideas." Their whole approach to the Bible is based on this kind of spiritualization.

(2) The main emphasis of Unity is on health and prosperity. Personal salvation is ignored completely. That man needs to be saved is denied. Its emphasis is on this life now on earth, as it is in many liberal Protestant churches to day. It offers no hope for life after death.

(3) Perhaps one of the greatest dangers of the cult is the fact that many of its sentiments are both beautiful and true -as far as they go. So when someone hears the message of a Unity church, he often misguidedly thinks it is just a more "practical" approach to "Christianity."

(4) You need to emphasize that the gospel is of grace, not of works. This is essential because of Unity's insistence that man is part of God-as a drop of water is a part of a great ocean. Therefore, according to Unity, man just needs to recognize who he is- part of God-possessing goodness and deserving of God's favor.

(5) Like the Christian Scientists, disciples of Unity don't like to think about sin and its punishment. They need to understand the gospel.

(6) Those who believe in Unity doctrine are usually so intent on looking for the good in man that they will not admit to the presence of any evil. Sometimes you might have to bring them to face reality by a question such as, "Do you think the brutal slaughter of six million Jews under the direction of Hitler was a GOOD thing?" Or, "Do you think a man is showing God-like qualities when he steals, lies, and murders?" (7) I am glad the Lord has given us the Bible, which is a sharp, two-edged sword, and which can penetrate the heart of man and bring in the light of the gospel. Without the power of the gospel from the Word of God, no one could be saved, including those under the teachings of Unity.

CHAPTER XVIII—Mormonism

History

Mormonism (also known as The Church of Jesus Christ of Latter-Day Saints) was organized in 1830 in Fayette, New York. An angel named Moroni was supposed to have appeared to Joseph Smith, Jr., revealing to him the place where golden plates were buried which contained the history of ancient America.

Also, according to Mormon belief, Smith received a pair of special eyeglasses (called "Urim and Thummim") which turned the "reformed-Egyptian characters" of the plates into English. Smith had a friend copy down the writing on the plates as he (Smith) read it to him. This later became the Book of Mormon, which is claimed by the Mormons to be an additional "revelation" for these latter days. They say it is as authoritative and inspired as the Bible.

In the early days of its history the members of the group were forced to migrate from one part of the country to another. With their pagan teaching of polygamy and frequent charges of a criminal nature against their leaders, the followers were pushed from "pillar to post." Joseph and his brother, Hyrum, were finally shot to death by an angry mob while they were awaiting trial in jail.

Today the Mormons are divided into two groups: The Church of Jesus Christ of Latter-Day Saints, who followed Brigham Young after Smith's death, and the Reorganized Church of Jesus Christ of Latter-Day Saints, composed of those who gave their support to Smith's son instead of to Brigham Young. Those who followed Young are the larger of the two.

Their Doctrine versus the Bible

(1) They have added to the Word of God. They claim other equally inspired books are The Book of Mormon, The Doctrine and Covenants, and The Pearl of Great Price.

Scripture warns against adding to what God has said. "Add thou not unto His Words, lest He reprove thee, and thou be found a liar" (Proverbs 30:6). "For I testify unto every man that heareth the words of the prophecy of this book, if any man (including Joseph Smith) shall add unto these things, God shall add unto him the plagues that are written in this book" (Revelation 22:18).

(2) They teach salvation by works. In the Articles of Faith of the Mormon Church it is stated, "The sectarian dogma of justification by faith alone has exercised an influence for evil since the early days of Christianity" (1925 ed., p. 479).

"Salvation" to the Mormons is received through following a system of rules. Their requirements for salvation are:

Belief in Christ
Public Confession
Water Baptism
Laying on of Hands
Obedience to the Ordinances of the Church.

How different this man-made system is from God's way of saving man through the Lord Jesus Christ. John 1:12 says, "As many as received Him, to them gave He power (the right) to become the sons of God, even to THEM THAT BELIEVE ON HIS NAME."

(3) They believe Christ was created... in the same way that we were created. They teach men existed in eternity past as spirit beings. Later on we were given physical bodies. Christ was simply another spirit being before He came to earth.

If Christ is only one of us, what would that make us? Their book A Compendium of the Doctrines of the Gospel answers the question for us. "God Himself was once as we are now, and is an exalted Man, and sits enthroned in yonder heavens" (p. 190). This teaching is complete blasphemy against the clear teaching of the Word of God. A religion such as this could never be considered "Christian" by the Lord Jesus Christ!

SUGGESTIONS FOR WITNESSING TO MORMONS

(l) When speaking to one, always get him to agree to use only the Bible in the conversation. You can do this with a statement like: "Since you believe the Bible is God's Word, and I do, too; and since I do not believe the Book of Mormon is God's Word, let's confine our conversation to what the BIBLE says. After all, if both books are from God, they certainly wouldn't contradict one another." He will usually agree to this. Once he does, you can make much better progress. Because the Mormon is not familiar with the plan of salvation, it will be good news to him.

(2) Do not allow the Mormon to leave a passage until he has faced up to it. This is especially important if he tries to quote from the Book of Mormon to prove a point which is contradictory to Scripture.

(3) Remember that the issue is still "grace and works." Don't let the conversation deviate from this if at ALL possible. The more you talk about other things, the more time it will take to lead him to the Lord, and the more difficult it will be to do so.

(4) If the Mormon speaks of some strange doctrine that may get your curiosity up, just let it drop... or you will find he will be doing all the talking and you won't be covering the plan of salvation.

(5) It is always important as you are witnessing to be praying for God to give you wisdom and to direct the thoughts of the unsaved person toward the gospel. "If any of you lack wisdom, let him ask of God, that giveth to all men liberally, and upbraideth not; and it shall be given him" (James 1:5).

"Now thanks be unto God, which always causeth us to triumph in Christ, and maketh manifest the savour of His knowledge by us in every place" (II Corinthians 2:14).

CHAPTER XIX—UNDERSTANDING THE TWO NATURES

Much confusion arises from improper teaching of the two natures. As a soulwinner, you need to understand this subject, not only so you can answer the questions of others, but also so you can effectively live your own life for the Lord. Without understanding what the Scriptures teach on this subject you will often be confused, doubtful, anxious, and unable to maintain your faithful, effective witnessing.

Lack of understanding of the two natures brings about questions like the following:

(1) Does a truly saved person sin any more?
(2) Can I lose my salvation if I keep sinning?
(3) What happens to a Christian when he sins?
(4) How can a Christian have the power really to serve the Lord?

Study this chapter carefully, looking up the verses in your Bible, and you will discover the answers to these questions.

The new birth is provided by God when a man by sincere faith accepts the payment that the Lord Jesus Christ made for him on the cross. It is not a process or a result of good works. It is not water baptism. It is a birth. John 3: 5 states a man must be born of water. This is specifically speaking of the Holy Spirit. This is living water, not H20, and is referred to throughout the book of John as the Holy Spirit (John 4:11, 14; John 7:38, 39).

The first birth is of the flesh. The second birth is of the Spirit (John 3:6). These two are completely separate, and nothing of the birth of the flesh has anything to do with the second birth which is of the Spirit. The flesh birth is from fleshly parents. The spirit birth is from God Himself, who is a Spirit (John 1:12, 13). Never confuse the two by thinking the flesh can do something to bring on the spirit birth. Like reproduces like, and flesh can reproduce only flesh. Only spirit can give birth to spirit.

The new birth does not come from prayers; neither is speaking in an unknown jargon proof of it. The Holy Spirit is guaranteed by God to all who believe (John 7:38, 39; II Cor. 1:22). The Holy Spirit is always spoken of as a gift of God, not coming by man's efforts (Rom. 5:5).

The Apostles never tried to "pray through" or work for the Holy Spirit. They were commanded to wait for the Holy Spirit in Jerusalem, and God would send the Holy Spirit to them (Acts 1:4, 5). They waited in Jerusalem, and after the 50 days that were prophesied were fulfilled, the Holy Spirit came upon them (Acts 2:1-17). The promise was given to all who would receive the Lord Jesus Christ as their Saviour-not to a few. "And it shall come to pass in the last days, saith God, I will pour out of my Spirit upon all flesh" (Acts 2: 17). This was referring to all who would receive the Lord Jesus Christ as their Saviour.

When a person is saved, a man's carnal desires of the flesh do not change or improve one iota. They remain the same. Flesh is flesh, and it remains that way (John 3:6). Much unscriptural teaching and confusion come from thinking the old nature should get better after salvation, and when people still see sin in their lives, it brings great doubt as to whether or not their conversion was real, or whether or not they have lost their salvation, etc.

I John 3: 9 says, "Whosoever is born of God doth not commit sin: for His seed remaineth in him: and he cannot sin, because he is born of God." Beyond any question, this verse teaches that the new birth of the Spirit never commits any sin. There are other verses that teach the old nature never gets any better but remains evil, such as Romans 7:18, "For I know that in me (that is, in my flesh) dwelleth no good thing: for to will is present with me, but how to perform that which is good I find not."

The Bible teaches that the old nature doesn't change, but it can be controlled by the power of the Holy Spirit who indwells all believers. Whether the new nature or the old nature will control the individual depends entirely upon the person's decision of which nature he will nurture and allow to rule. Galatians 5:16, "This I say then, Walk in the Spirit, and ye shall not fulfil the lust of the flesh." The Greek meaning of the word "walk" is to be "responsive, controlled, and guided." In other words, be responsive to the Spirit, controlled by the Spirit, and guided by the Spirit, and you will not be controlled by the flesh. The desires of the flesh will still be present, but you will not be controlled by them.

Please notice that this verse is not saying, "Do not fulfill the lusts of the flesh, and you will be spiritual." Many people equate a pious, negative life with being a really spiritual person. Many people in this category become hyper-critical and yet never lead a soul to the Lord.

There is a continual battle between the old and new natures. "For the flesh lusteth against the Spirit, and the Spirit against the flesh: and these are contrary the one to the other; so that ye cannot do the things that ye would" (Gal. 5:17).

If you want the new nature to be victorious in your life, you must feed and exercise that nature. Remember, your old nature has been fed and exercised all your life until you were saved. Your old nature will rule your life unless you feed and exercise your new nature regularly.

For example, in a boxing match the fighter who is the better trained and the stronger wins. They never match two men in a ring, one being very large and strong and the other being small and weak... because it would not even be a contest.

The fruit (result) of being controlled by the Spirit is described in Gal. 5:22, 23, "But the fruit of the Spirit is love, joy, peace, longsuffering, gentleness, goodness, faith, meekness, temperance; against such there is no law."

The fruit (result) of being controlled by the flesh is described in Galatians 5:19-21, "Now the works of the flesh are manifest, which are these; adultery, fornication, uncleanness, lasciviousness, idolatry, witchcraft, hatred, variance, emulations, wrath, strife, seditions, heresies, envyings, murders, drunkenness, revellings, and such like: of the which I tell you before, as I have also told you in time past, that they which do such things shall not inherit the kingdom of God." The last phrase in verse 21 points out that no evil works can enter heaven, but that they are the results of a man being under the control of the old nature. Only righteousness enters into heaven, which comes only from the new birth. The new birth never sins but is incorruptible (I Peter 1:23).

It is difficult for people to understand clearly that heaven is a perfect place and only a perfectly righteous person can enter therein; but this righteousness is not a result of man's works, but is a result of a perfect righteousness that is given to man through the new birth. I Cor. 6:9, 10 tells us that no sin shall enter heaven... but verse 11 tells us how we are washed and justified in the Name of the Lord Jesus Christ. Then, after a person is saved, he has the power to serve the Lord and to be a witness (Acts 1:8).

There is no SECRET to having a "victorious Christian life." It is very clearly taught in the Bible. II Tim. 2:4 tells us that "No man that warreth entangleth himself with the affairs of this life: that he may please Him who hath chosen him to be a soldier." To effectively live your life for the Lord, your life must be disciplined-to include the things of the Lord-and to leave out the things of the world. Colossians 3:2 tells us to "Set your affection on things above, not on things on the earth."

When we really keep in mind that people are lost and going to hell, and that we have been entrusted with the gospel message that will lead them to the Lord and heaven, it is not so difficult to determine that our lives are going to COUNT for the Lord. It is an every day, every moment decision. Every time you say "YES" and obey the Lord, instead of saying "NO" and disobeying Him, you are "spiritual"-controlled by the Holy Spirit. And this is how to be a happy, productive child of God.

CHAPTER XX—UNDERSTANDING PREDESTINATION

BIBLICAL DOCTRINE: "God is absolutely sovereign, and in His sovereignty gave man a free will to accept or reject the salvation that He has provided. It is God's will that all would be saved and that none should perish. God foreknows but does not predetermine any man to be condemned. God permits man's destiny to depend upon man's choice" (Florida Bible College Doctrinal Statement, Point Four).

I Tim. 2:4 tells us that God would have all men to be saved and come to the knowledge of the truth. God does not predetermine who will believe and who will not believe, but God predetermined what will HAPPEN to the believers and to the unbelievers.

The father who asks the son to mow the yard may have predetermined that if he does, he will reward him, and if he doesn't, he will chasten him. God explains our salvation in this same way... that the choice of our salvation is up to us, but He has predetermined the RESULTS of our choices.

Acts 10:34; Eph. 6:9; Col. 3:25; Rom. 2:11; and II Chron. 19:7 all point out clearly that God is no respecter of persons and does not choose one to be saved and one to be lost, but loves all alike. This is certainly clear in John 3:16, "For God so loved the world that He gave His only begotten Son, that whosoever believeth in Him should not perish, but have everlasting life."

II Thess. 2:13 says, "But we are bound to give thanks alway to God for you, brethren beloved of the Lord, because God hath from the beginning chosen you to salvation THROUGH sanctification of the Spirit AND belief of the truth." We are made pure and holy by sanctification of the Spirit. Look up the word "holy" in the Strong's Concordance, #37 in the Greek New Testament, and you will find it means to be made "holy, pure, and blameless." God chose those that believe the truth to be sanctified by the Spirit. But He did NOT choose WHO would believe the truth!

Eph. 1:4 is addressed to those who have received Christ as their Saviour and says that God predetermined all BELIEVERS to be before Him, holy, and without blame. Fatalists believe that this verse is teaching God chooses some to be saved. But the entire epistle of Ephesians is written to those who are already saved (Eph. 1:1), and verse four specifically says this is to those who are already "in Him"- believers who are in Christ. Ephesians 1:13 tells us we heard the Word of truth first; then, by believing, we were sealed with the Holy Spirit.

Romans 8: 29 tells us more about God's foreknowledge, "For whom He did foreknow, He also did predestinate to be conformed to the image of His Son, that He might be the firstborn among many brethren." Some take this out of its context and say God chose some and made them to be conformed to the image of His Son, instead of realizing that God FOREKNEW those who would believe and predestinated the BELIEVERS to be conformed to the image of His Son. He did not predetermine WHO would believe. He predetermined what would happen to those who did believe. I Peter 1: 2 also tells us we are chosen according to God's foreknowledge of who would believe.

God has a faculty that people do not have. He can see the future perfectly. Perhaps this is because God is "timeless," and therefore is actually living in the future as well as in the present. If we could see into the future and know exactly what things would take place, we could tell people what would happen in the future... not that we would MAKE these things happen... but simply that we would KNOW what will happen.

God does not "decide" who will be saved. God does not "make" any one believe, even though He wants all to believe and be saved. But God, since He can see the future, knows who will believe and who will not believe. Long before I was ever born, God knew I would decide to trust Christ as my Saviour. But this "foreknowledge" of His did not CAUSE me to trust Christ as my Saviour.

In Matt. 23:37 we find that Christ looked over Jerusalem and said that He would have gathered them together many times, but the people would not receive Him. God did not make these people reject Him. In fact, it is God who is desiring them to accept Him. But it is the people who would not, by their own free will and choice.

Our salvation comes through OUR OWN belief. The Bible is full of Scriptures that point this out. Rom. 1:16, "For I am not ashamed of the gospel of Christ, for it is the power of God unto salvation to every one that BELIEVETH...." I Cor. 1:21, "For after that in the wisdom of God the world by wisdom knew not God, it pleased God by the foolishness of preaching to save them that BELIEVE." John 3: 18, "He that BELIEVETH ON HIM is not condemned: but he that BELIEVETH NOT is condemned already, because he hath not BELIEVED in the Name of the only begotten Son of God." See also Habakkuk 2:4; Luke 7:50; Matt. 15:28; Psalm 119:173; Jude, vv. 10, 16-19; Psalm 119:30; Gen. 6:12; Isa. 29:13; John 17:8; Hos. 4:6; Isa. 55:1.

II Peter 3:9 says God is "not willing that ANY should perish, but that ALL should come to repentance (change of mind)."

Luke 2:10-The angel told us that the good news would be to ALL people, not to a limited number.

FATALIST POSITION: Many fatalists teach that faith is a gift of God and that God would have to "give" you the faith in order for you to believe. But God gives everyone the ability to believe (faith). Man may exercise this ability in any direction. Man can have faith in Buddha, Mohammed, or any cult or sect... and by their same definition, this would be a God-given ability to believe (faith) in Buddha, etc., as well as Christ. The faith we placed in the Lord Jesus Christ to save us COULD have been placed in Mohammed. The CHOICE was left up to us.

Some fatalists use the "sign theory," trying to take contradictory statements and make them seem not to be contradictory. They place a sign over heaven saying, "Whosoever will may come." But after you get to heaven you see the reverse side of the sign which says, "Chosen in Him before the foundation of the world." (This, of course, is only a partial quotation of Scripture, and you just studied the answer to these-the answer is that BELIEVERS are chosen to be before the Lord, holy and blameless someday.) The fatalists say, "We do not understand it," and they think this explains it.

This "sign theory" cannot be true because you would have to place the same sign over hell in the same way, saying, "Whosoever rejects Christ goes to hell," and on the other side of the sign you would have to place, "Chosen to go to hell from the foundation of the world." The reverse side of this sign would be just as unscriptural as the reverse side of the one over heaven.

IN CONCLUSION: "WHOSOEVER shall call upon the Name of the Lord shall be saved" (Romans 10:133).

Praise the Lord that our God is truly one of love, and who offers, "And ye shall seek Me, and find Me, when ye shall search for Me with all your heart" (Jeremiah 29: 13). Psalm 107:9 says, "For He satisfieth the longing soul, and filleth the hungry soul with goodness."

There is no person who has ever lived on the face of the earth that the Holy Spirit of God hasn't worked with continually, showing the person the truths of God. Christ in John 16:8 says the Holy Spirit convicts the world (every body) of sin, of righteousness, and of judgment. No one can stand before God and say he didn't have the opportunity to hear the truth. "For the invisible things of Him from the creation of the world are clearly seen, being understood by the things that are made, even His eternal power and Godhead; so that they are WITHOUT EXCUSE" (Rom. 1:20). "For the grace of God that bringeth salvation hath appeared to ALL MEN" (Titus 2:11).

CHAPTER XXI—HELPFUL HINTS

1. AIDS TO MEMORIZING SCRIPTURE VERSES

Use 3x5 file cards, writing the verse on one side and the address on the other. This way you can go through the addresses to see if you know the verses, and through the verses to see if you know the addresses.

As you learn your verses, try quoting them as frequently as possible, and you will implant them more firmly in your mind. It is a well-known fact that when you compound reading, hearing, and speaking in the learning process, your retention will be progressively increased. Just listening or reading alone cannot give you skill and effectiveness in USING your knowledge. You must PRACTICE. It is well said that "practice makes perfect that which you practice."

A periodic review of your memory verses is a good idea, even for the ones you feel you know quite well. If you have your 3x5 cards handy, you can make good use of time that perhaps you would otherwise waste... waiting for a bus, sitting in the beauty shop, etc.

Work toward knowing the verses so well that you can quote them immediately upon hearing the address, a portion of the verse, or subject material which the verse could answer or deals with.

Be able to quote them with almost no effort at all. In this way you can quote the verse to the person and actually be free to be thinking of what you will say next, or to be sensing the person's reaction to it. The value of being able to do this is great.

2. DON'T ARGUE

Winning an argument might make you feel good-until you realize that doing so might result in the person's ego being so hurt that his judgment is impaired and he won't trust Christ as his Saviour.

One reason why so few people have a very fruitful soul winning ministry is that they are just plain inconsiderate of the feelings of the person to whom they are witnessing.

It is TRUE that the lost person must repent. He MUST change his mind and come to see that anything he has been trusting in other than Christ alone for his salvation cannot save him.

Christ IS "THE way, THE truth, and THE life." And as you present the plan of salvation the lost person will discover that he has been wrong in his preconceived idea.

Because of this, BE KIND. You know how bad YOU feel when YOU are wrong about something, so remember the lost person also has feelings, and take great care in HOW you show him the truth of the gospel and the error of anything else.

(Of course, this should never involve a compromise in doctrine. This is just using good sense. Ephesians 4:15 says to speak "the TRUTH in LOVE." One does not exclude the other. They should go hand in hand.)

If you have ever been in the position of talking to many people and getting to know their problems, you have already discovered how very lonely and hungry for love and understanding people really are.

The soulwinner who realizes this and will really be kind and considerate of the lost will not only win many souls, but will win life-long friends as well.

3. Using Illustrations

As you read through the Gospels you cannot help noticing our Lord's frequent use of illustrations. They are very valuable in making your points clear and understandable (as well as more interesting) to the person. If we will notice several things about Christ's illustrations and apply them to our own, we will find our illustrations very effective.

A. They should be about subjects familiar to the person.

B. As much as possible, they should be concrete, rather than abstract, forming a picture in the person's mind.

C. They should be short and to the point, not taking up too much time. Don't get carried away with illustrations to the point that they usurp the proper place of Scripture in your presentation. Always bear in mind that your illustrations are a means to an end-to throw additional light upon the Scriptures-and not an end in themselves.

D. Never use illustrations with shady tones. This certainly would defeat your purpose of getting the person's mind more on the Scriptures and the Lord Jesus Christ. It will cause the person to think less of you and less of your message.

E. When you use an illustration from a book or from a person's life, don't tell it as if it happened in your own life. Although examples out of your own experience will naturally carry a certain added interest, it is not necessary that they be so. Just don't lie about it.

4. Look Nice

Would you expect the representative of a life insurance company to look neat, clean, and nicely dressed? How long do you think you would listen to his sales talk if he were shabby, dirty, and needed a shave?

Would an ambassador of the United States be representing our country properly as he met to discuss important issues with the ambassador of an important country if he wore an unpressed suit, had grease stains on his tie, needed a haircut, and had "B.O."?

Would the receptionist of a large, important company have her job long if she came to work and interviewed clients with her hair all messed up, her nail polish peeling off, yesterday's supper still in her teeth, and her dress needing ironing?

Of Course Not!

As Christians, as ambassadors for the King of Kings, desiring to influence people to receive the gift of eternal life, we certainly should look as clean, neat, and attractive as we possibly can.

With careful planning there is no reason why a person should not be able to have an adequate wardrobe even though he is not a millionaire. This doesn't mean you must have every new "fad" that comes along in your closet, but you should make every effort to be reasonably stylish in accordance with the people you come into contact with.

It is absolutely inexcusable to irritate people with "B.O." and bad breath. Today's provisions against these things are too readily available for you to be offensive here. There is no substitute for cleanliness.

5. Sincere Compliments

Often just one compliment will so soften a person that he will relax and open up to the gospel right away.

When witnessing to a brilliant person, let him know you know he is smart. Compliment, for instance, a good lawyer on his abilities, or a great physician on his accomplishments. And remember, you do not have to study law to witness to a lawyer, or medicine to witness to a doctor. The gospel is your power.

6. Agree

When a person is right, agree with him. Agree with him vehemently whenever possible. And when you must disagree, please do so in as pleasant a way as you can... as it has been said, many Christians are "dispensationally correct, but dispositionally wrong." The Bible says "be ye kind one to another."

7. Use "The Hand Gesture"

This method of securing the person's attention and then explaining the gospel to him as you use a gesture is fully pictured and developed in Chapter 23. This is one of the most effective things we have ever found to make the gospel clear and understandable to the lost. Use it!

8. Too Many Verses

Because we love the Word of God and find many verses so precious to us, we sometimes find ourselves using so many verses with a lost person that he gets confused. When one verse clarifies the point, leave it there. If you need another verse, fine; use another one. But usually the person's problem will not so much be one of needing many verses, but rather that he does not understand or believe the verse you have just shown him.

9. Using Questions

Aristotle was famous for teaching by means of asking questions of his students. In this way the student could think out the truth of what he was trying to get across better than if he just lectured them. This is also true in witnessing. If a verse says, "whosoever believeth in him should not perish, but have everlasting life," you might ask: "Does this verse say, whosoever works, and joins the church, and pays the tithe will not perish? Does this verse say that those who believe will have life until they start sinning again?" Questions will help the person think WITH you about the Scriptures.

10. Tell The Truth

If you are asked a question which you cannot answer at the moment, don't bluff it. Say you don't know, and offer to find the answer and give it to him at a later date. In your own notebook you might want to keep a list of questions and their answers which are difficult for you to answer, along with explanations of passages that are difficult for you to explain. In time, after experience, you will find greater ease even in answering these.

11. He Doesn't Understand What You Are Saying

If the person doesn't grasp what you are trying to put across, instead of implying that he is "stupid," why not rather suggest that perhaps you haven't made it clear enough? This will let him "save face" and you will be able to continue your ministry with him.

12. "Christian" America

Since the majority of people in America feel that they are Christians, it isn't good to ask a person if he is a Christian. Most people will say "yes" to this even if they are unsaved, and then you have to prove them wrong before you can lead them to the Lord.

Rather, ask questions like, "What do you think you have to do to go to heaven?" or "Do you know where you are going when you die?" Their answers to questions like these will give you a better idea of what to say to lead them to the Lord.

13. Learning From Others

If you hear your preacher use a good illustration... if you see another soulwinner using a particular method in his soulwinning... if you find someone uses a particular phrase which increases his effectiveness in making the gospel clear... don't be afraid to do the same.

When a man is leading people to the Lord, try doing what he does. In I Cor. 4:16 the Apostle Paul urged his children in the faith to follow his Christian example.

The important thing isn't who originated this or that... the important thing is doing everything we can to make the plan of salvation understandable to the lost. All the glory belongs to the Lord.

14. Suggestions In Witnessing To Members Of Cults

A. They are still people. Just treat them as you would any other persons in need of salvation. The gospel is the power of God unto salvation to everyone (including the cultists) if they will believe. Try not to give the appearance of "shock" if you discover some "odd" thing they believe.

B. Often people are attracted to a cult or false religion because of the interest shown to them by the members of that group. Christians ought to show genuine love and concern for people and be all the more careful to "speak the truth in love."

C. The disciples of cults are usually quite zealous about their beliefs and love to talk. Let them. Don't be rude. Listen attentively so that when they are through with the presentation you may be better equipped to meet their needs in your presentation of the gospel.

D. Remember that these people are blinded by Satan. "In whom the god of this world hath blinded the minds of them which believe not..." (II Cor. 4:4). The entrance of God's Word will give them the light they need (Psalm 119: 130).

E. Be careful not to get off onto "side issues" which are of no profit to the person's salvation. Stay with the main issue which, in most cases, will still be "grace and works."

CHAPTER XXII—LITERATURE: RECOMMENDED READING LIST

These recommendations are not intended to be exhaustive. Thousands of books written by Christians have much good information in them, but we are listing some which we have found especially helpful in particular areas. If we have left out one of your favorite books, please do not feel we are inferring it isn't good.

Since only the Bible is the inspired Word of God, no other book is 100% perfect. There may be portions of some books recommended here that you may feel contain some error.

Perhaps there are some things in this book you will disagree with. We must learn how to read a book or hear a preacher, benefiting from the good information and disregarding the poor. Use the Scriptures as the criteria and just pray earnestly and endeavor to keep your own message true to the Word of God.

We believe you will find these books greatly helpful to you and those in your care, under the following categories.

SALVATION

All About Repentance	Seymour	Harvest House	Full Assurance	Ironside	CrossReach Publications
Shall Never Perish	Strombeck	Moody Press	So Great Salvation	Strombeck	Moody Press
The Gift of God	Seymour	Grace Publishing Co.			

CHRISTIAN EVIDENCES

A Coffer of Jewels	Rice	Sword Of The Lord	A Lawyer Examines the Bible	Linton	Baker Book House
A Scientific Investigation of the Old Testament	Wilson	Moody Press	Can I Trust the Bible?	Symposium	Moody Press
Escape from Reason	Schaeffer	InterVarsity Press	General Biblical Introduction	Miller	Word-Bearer Press
Know Why You Believe	Little	Scripture Press	Set Forth Your Case	Pinnock	The Craig Press
The Harmony of Science and Scripture	Rimmer	Eerdmans			
The God Who Is There	Schaeffer	InterVarsity Press			

SCIENCE AND THE BIBLE

Did Man Just Happen?	Criswell	Zondervan	Evolution, Fact or Theory?	Reno	Moody Press

Studies in the Bible and Science	Morris	Baker Book House	The Bible and Modern Science	Morris	Moody Press
The Theory of Evolution and the Facts of Science	Rimmer	Eerdmans	Why We Believe in Creation	Meldau	Christian Victory Pub. Co.

Christian Growth

A Spiritual Clinic	Sanders	Moody Press	Balancing the Christian Life	Ryrie	Moody Press
Disciplined by Grace	Strombeck	Moody Press	Effective Bible Study	Voss	Zondervan
Now That I Believe	Cook	Moody Press	Prayer: Asking and Receiving	Rice	Sword of the Lord
Ready, Set, Grow	Seymour	Harvest House			

Doctrine

Bible Doctrines	Cambron	Zondervan	Dispensational Truth	Larkin	Larkin Estate
Holiness: the False and the True	Ironside	CrossReach Publications	Major Bible Themes	Chafer	Zondervan
Rightly Dividing the Word of Truth	Scofield	Loizeaux Brothers	Systematic Theology	Chafer	Dallas Seminary
The Hungry Inherit	Hodges	Moody Press	The Sovereign God	Seymour	Harvest House

Witnessing

Golden Path to Successful Personal Soulwinning	Rice	Sword of the Lord	Great Personal Workers	Whitesell	Moody Press
Hand Gathered Fruit	Last	Christian Literature Crusade	Soul-Winner's Fire	Rice	Moody Press
The Master Plan of Evangelism	Coleman	Revell			

Religions and Cults

All About Tongues	Seymour	Harvest House	Authors of Confusion	Gustafson	Grace Publishers
Chaos of Cults	VanBaalen	Eerdmans	False Doctrines	Rice	Sword of the Lord
Foxe's Book of Martyrs	Foxe	Revell	Heresies Exposed	Irvine	Loizeaux
Jehovah of the Watchtower	Martin & Klann	Zondervan	Kingdom of the Cults	Martin	Bethany Fellowship
Neo-Evangelicalism	Woodbridge	Bob Jones Univ. Press	So What's the Difference?	Ridenour	Gospel Light Publishers
The Christian and the Cults	Martin	Zondervan	The Christian Science Myth	Martin & Klann	Zondervan
The Coming World Church	(various authors)	Back to the Bible	The Maze of Mormonism	Martin & Klann	Zondervan
The Modern Tongues Movement	Gromacki	Presbyterian & Reformed Publishing Co.			
The New Evangelicalism	Starr	Cornerstone Baptist Church	The New Neutralism	Ashbrook	Calvary Bible Church

General

How to Win Friends and Influence People	Carnegie	Simon & Schuster			

CHAPTER XXIII—Illustration Illustrated

A person can understand something much better if he can SEE what you are talking about as well as HEAR you. You have heard it said that "a picture is worth a thousand words."

Also, when a person is LOOKING at something, you have a better chance of explaining it without being interrupted.

The "visual aid" gesture, pictured step-by-step below, has been found EXTREMELY VALUABLE in making the plan of salvation clear and understandable to the lost—especially on the point that the Lord Jesus Christ has made a complete payment for sin.

1.) Let this hand represent you and me.

2.) Let this wallet represent our sin. We all have sin on us.
Romans 3:23

3.) God loves us.
John 3:16

4.) But He hates our sin.
Psalm 4:5

5.) Our sin separates us from God. We cannot get rid of our sin by our good works.
Isaiah 59:2; Ephesians 2:8-9

6.) If we pay for our sin, we will have to pay for it by death and hell.
Romans 6:23

7.) Let this hand represent the Lord Jesus Christ. He had no sin. He was perfect.
II Corinthians 5:21

8.) Christ voluntarily took our sin upon Himself.
I Peter 2:24

9.) He paid for our sin by dying in our place on the cross. Our sin is no longer on us, because He took it and paid for it. He gives us His righteousness.
II Corinthians 5:21

10.) You can know you have eternal life when you, by faith, accept this payment Christ made for you.
I John 5:13

More Evangelism Titles from CrossReach Publications

Words to Winners of Souls
Horatius Bonar

"How much more would a few good and fervent men effect in the ministry than a multitude of lukewarm ones!" Such was the remark of œcolampadius, the swiss reformer,—a man who had been taught by experience, and who has recorded that experience for the benefit of other churches and other days. It is a remark, however, the truth of which has been but little acknowledged and acted on; nay, whose importance is to this day unappreciated even where its truth is not denied.

Open Air Preaching
William Evans

This is seen by the indisputable fact that the greatest and most influential preachers and teachers of the ages past, and the age in which we now live, have made constant use of it.

The messages of the prophets were delivered in the open air. God's call to the prophet was: "Go, proclaim these words in the streets of the city" (Jer. 11:6). The sublime evangelical predictions of Isaiah; the mournful dirges of Jeremiah; the symbolical and picturesque visions of Ezekiel—all these, for the most part, were announced in the streets of the great cities of Jerusalem and Babylon. Throughout the streets of Nineveh resounded the warning voice of the prophet Jonah. The message of Micah, Nahum, and the rest of the minor prophets was, without question, "a song of the winds." Nehemiah's great revival sermon—a sermon which resulted in an almost national revival—was preached in the street of Jerusalem, close to the water-gate. (Neh. 8:1, 3.) The open-air worker and preacher of to-day, then, is in "the goodly order of the prophets."

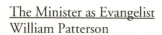

How to Use Tracts in Evangelism
H. W. Pope

The indiscriminate use of tracts by those whose zeal exceeds their wisdom has led many good people to have a strong prejudice against them. The character of the tracts used has also strengthened this prejudice. Some tracts are so antiquated as to be almost useless in the present age. They were good in their day, but their day has gone by. Others are so lacking in pith, point or power as to be of little value. To use a modern phrase, they do not "get there." Others still are so offensive in style as to defeat the very end for which they were written.

It is foolish, however, to allow prejudice against poor tracts to blind us to the value of good ones. And good ones can be had. The choicest thoughts of the best writers can now be found in leaflet form, and there is moral dynamite enough in some of them to shatter terribly the strongholds of Satan. Indeed, the Bible itself is only a collection of sixty-six little tracts bound in one volume; for, as someone has said, "holy men of God wrote small books on great subjects."

The Minister as Evangelist
William Patterson

The work of the Minister, according to the teaching of the New Testament, is threefold.

First, he is to feed the church of God—the babes, with the sincere milk of the Word; and those who are more advanced with the strong meat of its doctrines.

Second, he is to care for those over whom he has been placed as an overseer or under-shepherd. This twofold aspect of the work was very clearly brought out by our Savior, on that early morning when He stood by the Lake of Gennesaret and commanded Peter to feed the sheep and the lambs and to shepherd them. We are all agreed as to the importance of these two departments in connection with the minister's work; in fact, we can hardly overestimate the importance of building up Christian people in faith and in knowledge, and also in caring for them as the shepherd cares for the sheep, by leading them to the green pastures and the quiet waters.

Third, he is commanded to do the work of an Evangelist; in other words, to reach out after the unsaved and to bring into the fold those who are outside. This part of the work was surely referred to when Christ called the disciples and told them that, if they would follow Him, He would make them "fishers of men;" that as they had in the past drawn the fish out of the sea by the net, they would in the future draw men from the sea of iniquity to the rock of safety.

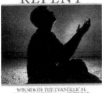

Except Ye Repent
H. A. Ironside

Fully convinced in my own mind that the doctrine of repentance is the missing note in many otherwise orthodox and fundamentally sound circles today, I have penned this volume out of a full heart. I hope and pray that God will be pleased to use it to awaken many of His servants to the importance of seeking so to present His truth as to bring men to the only place where He can meet them in blessing. That place is the recognition of their own demerit and absolute unworthiness of His least mercies and a new conception of His saving power for all who come to Christ as lost sinners, resting alone upon His redemptive work for salvation, and depending upon the indwelling Holy Spirit to make them victorious over sin's power in daily life.

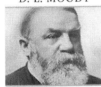

Why God Used D. L. Moody
R. A. Torrey

Dwight L. Moody. After our great generals, great statesmen, great scientists and great men of letters have passed away and been forgotten, and their work and its helpful influence has come to an end, the work of D. L. Moody will go on and its saving influence continue and increase, bringing blessing not only to every state in the Union but to every nation on earth. Yes, it will continue throughout the ages of eternity.

My subject is "Why God Used D. L. Moody," and I can think of no subject upon which I would rather speak. For I shall not seek to glorify Mr. Moody, but the God who by His grace, His entirely unmerited favour, used him so mightily, and the Christ who saved him by His atoning death and resurrection life, and the Holy Spirit who lived in him and wrought through him and who alone made him the mighty power that he was to this world. Furthermore: I hope to make it clear that the God who used D. L. Moody in his day is just as ready to use you and me, in this day, if we, on our part, do what D. L. Moody did, which was what made it possible for God to so abundantly use him.

The Gospel for Today
R. A. Torrey

The Gospel presented in these sermons is the same Gospel of a crucified Christ, a Saviour from the guilt of sin, and a risen Christ, a Saviour from the present power of sin, that we have been preaching throughout our entire ministry as pastor, and as evangelist in all parts of the world. We are certainly living in a New Day. The War and its after-results have worked a radical transformation in the ethical and religious as well as social and economic outlook of the minds of the men and women of the present day; nevertheless, we find that the same Gospel that was "the power of God unto salvation" before the War, and from the days of the Apostle Paul (Rom. 1:16), is the Gospel that men will listen to and yield to today. All of these new gospels, "The Social Gospel" with the rest, are proving utterly ineffective in saving individual men or in lifting up communities. The Real Gospel, when preached in the power of the Holy Spirit, produces the same effects in individual lives to-day, and in the transformation of families and communities, that it has produced throughout all the centuries since our Lord Jesus Christ died on the Cross of Calvary and rose again and ascended to the right hand of the Father and poured out His Holy Spirit upon His people. Practical results prove that that Gospel does not even need to be restated, though of course it is desirable to adapt the illustrations and method of argument to the thinking of our own day.

Revival Sermons
R. A. Torrey

REQUESTS have come from many quarters for the publication of some of the sermons which God has been pleased to so greatly use in Japan, China, Australia, Tasmania, New Zealand, India, England, and Scotland. This volume is published in response to this request. The author hopes that the sermons may be used as greatly in their printed form as they have been when spoken. The sermons when delivered, as here published, were taken down in shorthand, but have been carefully revised by the author. Each one of them has many sacred memories connected with it. When one of these sermons was delivered through an interpreter in a Japanese city, eighty-seven Japanese came forward and declared publicly their acceptance of Christ. After the delivery of another in Shanghai, a large number of Chinese men and women walked out from their places among their heathen companions and publicly professed their acceptance of Christ. On some occasions in Australia, Tasmania, and New Zealand, hundreds of men and women came forward and with their own lips publicly confessed their acceptance of Christ as their Saviour and their Lord. Reports of some of these sermons have been given in religious and secular papers, but these reports have been necessarily fragmentary and inaccurate, as they have never been revised by the author. I have abundant proof that even these unsatisfactory reports have done good, but it seems desirable that a full and accurate report of what I have said be given to the public.

What is the Gospel?
H. A. Ironside

It might seem almost a work of supererogation to answer a question like this. We hear the word, "Gospel" used so many times. People talk of this and of that as being "as true as the Gospel," and I often wonder what they really mean by it.

First I should like to indicate what it is not.

THE GOSPEL IS…

Not The Bible

In the first place, the Gospel is not the Bible. Often when I inquire, "What do you think the Gospel is?" people reply, "Why, it is the Bible, and the Bible is the Word of God." Undoubtedly the Bible is the Word of God, but there is a great deal in that Book that is not Gospel.

"The wicked shall be turned into Hell with all the nations that forget God." That is in the Bible, and it is terribly true; but it is not Gospel.

"It is a fearful thing to fall into the hands of the living God." That is in the Bible, but it is not the Gospel.

Our English word, "gospel" just means the "good spell," and the word "spell," is the old Anglo-Saxon word for, "tidings", the good tidings, the good news. The original word translated. "Gospel," which we have taken over into the English with little alteration is the word, "evangel," and it has the same meaning, the good news. The Gospel is God's good news for sinners. The Bible contains the Gospel, but there is a great deal in the Bible which is not Gospel.

Made in United States
Orlando, FL
09 April 2024

45608136R00067